# Cambridge Elements

Elements in Critical Heritage Studies
edited by
Kristian Kristiansen
*University of Gothenburg*
Michael Rowlands
*UCL*

# IN SEARCH OF NATIONAL ANCESTORS

## *Heritage, Identity, and Placemaking in China*

Shu-Li Wang
*Academia Sinica*

CAMBRIDGE
UNIVERSITY PRESS

Shaftesbury Road, Cambridge CB2 8EA, United Kingdom

One Liberty Plaza, 20th Floor, New York, NY 10006, USA

477 Williamstown Road, Port Melbourne, VIC 3207, Australia

314–321, 3rd Floor, Plot 3, Splendor Forum, Jasola District Centre,
New Delhi – 110025, India

103 Penang Road, #05–06/07, Visioncrest Commercial, Singapore 238467

Cambridge University Press is part of Cambridge University Press & Assessment,
a department of the University of Cambridge.

We share the University's mission to contribute to society through the pursuit of
education, learning and research at the highest international levels of excellence.

www.cambridge.org
Information on this title: www.cambridge.org/9781009582117

DOI: 10.1017/9781009582131



First published 2025

A catalogue record for this publication is available from the British Library

ISBN 978-1-009-58211-7 Hardback
ISBN 978-1-009-58214-8 Paperback
ISSN 2632-7074 (online)
ISSN 2632-7066 (print)

Cambridge University Press & Assessment has no responsibility for the persistence
or accuracy of URLs for external or third-party internet websites referred to in this
publication and does not guarantee that any content on such websites is, or will
remain, accurate or appropriate.

For EU product safety concerns, contact us at Calle de José Abascal, 56, 1°, 28003
Madrid, Spain, or email eugpsr@cambridge.org.

# In Search of National Ancestors

## Heritage, Identity, and Placemaking in China

Elements in Critical Heritage Studies

DOI: 10.1017/9781009582131
First published online: April 2025

Shu-Li Wang
*Academia Sinica*

**Author for correspondence:** Shu-Li Wang, shuliwang@gate.sinica.edu.tw

**Abstract:** This Element examines how international heritage discourses are internalized and reshaped in China, using the Yellow Emperor cults as a lens to explore broader themes of intangible heritage, religious resurgence, and identity construction. The central argument is that cultural heritage serves as a powerful tool for shaping new religious expressions and enabling Chinese localities to assert their uniqueness while redefining historical narratives. Through case studies of several localities across China, this Element illustrates how these regions engage in heritage competition by branding themselves with Yellow Emperor culture to shape their identities. The Element argues that the cult of the Yellow Emperor – a legendary figure – is empowered by nationalism, a local search for tradition, and religious revivals, and is further amplified by international discourses that reinforce national identity through heritage-making. Together, these forces drive the resurgence of ancestral cults and contribute to cultural identity formation in contemporary China.

**Keywords:** Yellow Emperor, Huangdi, religion, remote ancestor cults, name-cards, branding



ISBNs: 9781009582117 (HB), 9781009582148 (PB), 9781009582131 (OC)
ISSNs: 2632-7074 (online), 2632-7066 (print)

# Contents

## 1 Introduction

On March 28, 2017, just days before the grand ceremony honoring the Yellow Emperor (Huangdi 黃帝) in Xinzheng (新鄭) City, Henan (河南) Provin ce, I was invited by the Henan provincial government to attend an international forum on "Yellow Emperor Culture (黃帝文化)." During the accompanying banquet, I engaged in vibrant discussions with other attendees. A local official from Xiping (西平) County, Henan, shared ambitious plans to promote the legacy of Leizu (嫘祖), Huangdi's legendary first wife, and detailed an upcoming worship event dedicated to her. A scholar from Hubei (湖北) Province offered insights into their research on Shun (舜), one of ancient China's revered sage kings, while an official from Luyi (鹿邑) County emphasized the value of Laozi's (老子) teachings in establishing Luyi as a hub for "Laozi culture (老子文化)." Four days later, I traveled to Xi'an (西安) to participate in the Tomb Sweeping Festival honoring Huangdi in Shaanxi (陝西) Province. There, I attended a conference on "Huangdi culture," and met Mr. Huo, a senior scholar-official from Baoji (寶雞), Shaanxi. Mr. Huo ardently advocated for the legacy of Yandi (炎帝), the Flame Emperor, a legendary figure believed to have reigned alongside the Yellow Emperor. The prevailing narrative recounts the myth of Yandi's defeat by the barbarian Chiyou (蚩尤) and his subsequent alliance with Huangdi to overcome Chiyou in Zhuolu (逐鹿), Hebei (河北) Province – a pivotal event in the foundation of Chinese civilization. Today, Zhuolu commemorates these figures with a joint ceremony at a cultural park featuring three temples dedicated to Huangdi, Yandi, and Chiyou. In Shaanxi, I encountered other local officials, each overseeing ceremonies for a "deity," "ancestor," or "historical celebrity." After participating in two grand ceremonies honoring Huangdi within one week, I was struck by the feeling of stepping into a "garden of deities," where mythical figures from Chinese history seemed vividly alive.

The Chinese people are often referred to as the descendants of Yandi and Huangdi – collectively known as "Yan huang zisun (炎黃子孫)," meaning "descendants of the Yan Emperor and the Huang Emperor." The figures described earlier are central to China's foundational origin myths and are key to the mytho-historical narrative of the Three Sovereigns and Five Emperors (三皇五帝), a period traditionally believed to span from 2900 BC to 2100 BC. The estimated time span may vary depending on the sources consulted. This era is often regarded as the early phase of Chinese civilization, predating the establishment of dynastic China. The concept of "Yan huang zisun" and a linear, cohesive narrative of Chinese history emerged during the nineteenth century, a period marked by the transition from imperial China to a modern nation-state (Shen, 1997). Today, enthusiasm for common ancestors has experienced a resurgence, finding new expression within popular religion and the framework of cultural heritage, particularly under the influence of the United Nations Educational, Scientific and Cultural Organization (UNESCO). These mythological figures are now regarded as real ancestors to be honored by the government. The Chinese state has actively promoted ceremonies, festivals, and the construction of temples and monuments to commemorate these ancestors, officially recognizing them as part of China's intangible cultural heritage.

In the context of global heritage-making, it is crucial to avoid overgeneralizing or standardizing practices such as heritagization (Walsh, 1992) or UNESCOization (Berliner, 2012) across the world. Instead, critical heritage scholars should examine how different cultures respond to these global heritage trends and engage with the processes of globalization (Herzfeld, 2004). This raises important questions: How is cultural heritage situated within China, and how is it translated, transformed, and embedded in its contemporary sociopolitical, cultural, academic, and local contexts? Specifically, this Element investigates the role of the cults of the Yellow Emperor and other mythic ancestors in promoting nationalism in China. It examines how UNESCO's heritage discourse has been leveraged to support the revival of popular religion and traditional culture, even triggering new religious expressions. Furthermore, it explores how heritage discourse has been transformed and internalized in China, where localism and competition have emerged, leading to new forms of heritage rivalry. Focusing on the cult of the Yellow Emperor, this Element examines the rise of remote ancestor ceremonies in contemporary China, alongside the national enthusiasm for heritage listing and heritage-making, all set against the backdrop of China's search for national roots, where heritage discourse plays a central role in shaping both cultural and political landscapes. Despite criticism of the tangible–intangible distinction by critical heritage scholars, the inclusion of intangible heritage discourse has profoundly reshaped China's understanding of what constitutes heritage. This Element retains the term "intangible cultural heritage" (hereafter ICH).

This widespread revival of popular religion stands in significant contrast to Marxist atheist ideology. During Mao's regime [1949–1976], practices such as ancestor worship and temple visits were condemned as relics of feudal superstition. With the political loosening after the economic reforms in 1978, religious activities gradually resumed once again. Since the 1990s, there has been a resurgence in locally organized religious events, festivals, ancestral rites, and the construction of temples in every place, despite the relatively passive stance of the central government (see also Chau, 2006). However, in recent years, particularly since the 2000s, there has been a notable resurgence of these traditional customs, demonstrated through performances, folk dances, rituals, and religious practices, aimed at their promotion and preservation under the framework of ICH. In other words, aside from the general public, both governments and elites are becoming increasingly enthusiastic about promoting certain religious practices, albeit selectively, under official policies.

In today's China, there has been a significant resurgence in popular religion, evident in its growing prevalence and vitality (Chau, 2009; Johnson, 2017; Madsen, 2014). Among the diverse religious practices experiencing a revival, one notable trend is the emergence of large-scale "remote ancestral cults," a term I coined, which pay homage to legendary ancestors from distant epochs. These ceremonies actively involve various levels of governments, local officials, scholars, and numerous lineage organizations. Ancestor worship, once confined to familial or lineage settings, has now expanded into expansive communal rituals, increasingly managed by local governments in collaboration with tourism, commerce, and economic bureaus, drawing thousands of participants. Since the 1990s, my research has observed a gradual revitalization of Huangdi worship activities on a small scale in several places that are historically connected to Huangdi. Starting from 2000, government-led large-scale ceremonial events have been organized in Shaanxi, Henan, and Zhejiang (浙江), gaining recognition as national-level ICH. In addition to Huangdi, there has been a resurgence in the veneration of various "deified ancestors" such as Nüwa (女媧), Pangu (盤古), Fuxi (伏羲), Yandi, Dayu (大禹), Shun, Yao (堯), and other figures from the mythical period, across China. Although the temporal understanding of the concept of myth was introduced from Japan only in the late nineteenth century, debates surrounding these figures can be traced through various official historical and even "unorthodox" ancient texts throughout imperial China, due to their remoteness in time. In these contemporary new religious expressions, "mythical" and "legendary" figures from ancient Chinese culture are being rejuvenated through large-scale ancestor worship initiatives orchestrated by various local governments. Surprisingly, these large-scale ancestral cults are in the process of applying for various levels of heritage designation, signaling official recognition and endorsement of this practice of root worship and ancestral searching.

This zeal for rediscovering the national past and tradition, including religion – once dismissed as superstition or incompatible with modernity – is helping to foster a sense of national pride in China's long history, resonating with Benedict Anderson's (1983) concept of the "imagined community." Anderson (1983) emphasizes the "imagined" nature of national communities, where shared media, language, symbols, narratives, and cultural practices foster a sense of belonging among people who may never meet. These elements, many drawn from a nation's cultural heritage, contribute to the creation of a collective identity. Similarly, Michael Herzfeld (1991, 1997) has explored the concept of the "historical imaginary," in which certain historical events or figures are selectively remembered or forgotten to shape new narratives that suit present needs. In this view, history is not a static, fixed record but a dynamic and selective process through which societies reinterpret and reimagine their past to serve contemporary ideologies, power structures, or societal goals. Herzfeld's approach often focuses on how national identities and cultural practices are shaped by these reimaginings and appropriations of history. In this context, Herzfeld's work complements Benedict Anderson's theory of "imagined communities," where the shared narratives of the past (whether through print media, heritage, or collective memory) are instrumental in creating a sense of national cohesion. Additionally, Hobsbawm and Ranger (1983) examine the constructive nature of tradition, arguing that nationalism is closely tied to state formation and often involves the "invention" of traditions to promote unity. They highlight that much of what is considered "traditional" or "heritage" is actually a modern construct, shaped by historical forces and political agendas, thus challenging the view that traditions are inherently ancient or natural. While all four scholars view nationalism as a modern phenomenon, closely tied to the development of capitalism, print media, and the modern state, this Element also adopts a constructive approach to China's nation-building, highlighting the heritage boom with distinct Chinese characteristics that reflect the country's unique cultural landscape.

Building on this discussion, this Element analyzes various remote ancestral cults within the framework of contemporary nation-building, the continually selective use and construction of history, the transformation of tradition into heritage, and the ways in which heritage discourse has empowered this process, shaping a new heritage landscape in China. First, this Element argues that the cults of the Yellow Emperor are driven by strong nationalism, aiming to unify China's ethnicities and territorial integrity through a shared lineage based on blood and kinship. Recent leadership policies, such as the "China Dream," reinforce this emphasis by linking national revival to cultural heritage. The UNESCO heritage discourse echoes this sentiment, promoting the idea that heritage strengthens national identity. Together, these forces reinforce the resurgence of the Yellow Emperor cult as a tool for cultural and national consolidation. Heritage projects, like those reviving popular religion or traditional culture, seek to construct a cohesive national narrative by linking people to a shared past. These initiatives are playing a vital role in cultivating an imagined community (Anderson, 1983) in modern China, enabling individuals from diverse regions and backgrounds to connect with a unified historical identity.

Second, this Element observes a grassroots revival involving localities and individuals motivated by a search for national glory and a return to traditional culture. Local religious revivals, which have been emerging since the 1980s reform era, play a crucial role as communities reconnect with historical and cultural roots. As Stewart (2016, p. 300) asserts, "History thus takes shape in a hermeneutic circle consistent with Gadamer's (1994) idea of 'historically effected consciousness,'" wherein historical documents and heritage sites serve as repositories of social memory, integrated into individual cultural memory and actions.

Third, the Element identifies a new shift in China's heritage discourse, where localities – municipal, county, or provincial – shape their identities by aligning with legendary or historical figures and organizing public ceremonies to honor these ancestors. Handler (2011, p. 48) argues that "the contemporary world is organized by the model of the nation-state," in which nations are imagined to possess cultural properties that define their identity and legitimacy. Echoing Handler, this ethnography reveals how localities in China, much like individuals, construct distinct personalities through cultural heritage. In the context of globalization, as Sahlins (1999) suggests, "culturalism" positions local culture as a marker of unique identity, making it essential to examine how this local cultural production materializes. The construction of local identities will be discussed in Sections 4 and 5 through case studies in Huangling 黃陵 (Shaanxi), Xinzheng, Xinmin 新密, Lingbao 靈寶 (Henan), and Jinyun 縉紜 (Zhejiang).

Additionally, this resurgence is empowering a group of academic nationalists – including historians, archaeologists, and heritage makers – who are celebrating various ancestors and reshaping historical narratives. This academic nationalism is strengthening the cultural significance of the Yellow Emperor and other ancestral figures, contributing to the larger project of redefining China's past to suit contemporary national and cultural goals. My research on ancestral cult ceremonies found ongoing efforts by Chinese scholars to authenticate ancient texts and use archaeology to prove the historical existence of these figures, and this will be described in Section 5.

Drawing on ethnographic investigations conducted in China between 2017 and 2024, this Element examines the contemporary remembrances and appropriations of Huangdi as a common ancestor of the Chinese people, intertwined with an analysis of heritage-making processes in China. It transcends long-standing debates over Huangdi's historical or legendary status, traditionally examined by historians (Shen, 1997; Wang, 2002), and discussions on the construction of "Chinese" racial identity (Dikotter, 1992; Fei, 1989).

Instead, this Element primarily focuses on understanding how and why the revival of remote ancestral cults is influenced by national identity, local placemaking, and the heritage discourse. The Element uncovers the mechanisms behind cultural revivals and historical consciousness, driven by diverse actors and influenced by various factors in contemporary times. Historians continue to debate Huangdi's role as the ancestor of Chinese civilization, or even to question his existence, while archaeologists diligently seek material evidence that could provide insights into Huangdi's historical presence. Both efforts are supported by the state, aiming to establish a cohesive, unified Chinese ethnicity. Local governments vie to assert their legitimacy by organizing annual ceremonies, erecting monuments, and constructing temples dedicated to ancestor worship under the banner of "Huangdi culture." Beyond institutional efforts, this Element highlights how the desires of ordinary people for religious practices, ancestral veneration, and national unity contribute to the commemoration of this national ancestor. This is evident in the construction in his honor of temples, sculptures, and monuments that are gradually shaping new religious practices.

This revival reflects a nationwide resurgence of folk religious practices in public spaces following the Reform and Opening-Up era, and intriguingly promotes the phenomenon of Yellow Emperor Fever as ICH. While the pursuit of autochthonous common ancestors aims to build a kinship-based lineage among all Chinese people, including diverse ethnic minorities, there exists a dynamic tension between central and local authorities, as well as among localities in the scale and rights of holding Yellow Emperor ceremonies. I have observed a competitive spirit among localities, each striving to assert their "ownership" of these figures and the cultural heritage they embody. Driven largely by nationalism, this discourse on heritage aims to depict China as a historically profound nation. Yet, it also underscores a localized Chinese heritage discourse with regional competition, as localities strive to brand themselves with distinct cultural heritages, as argued in this Element.

## 2 Locating Religious Revivals in China within the Framework of Intangible Cultural Heritage

### National Cultural Revivals

Living in today's China, it is evident that history is prominently and grandly displayed, from public monuments and sculptures to historically themed shopping districts, theme parks, restored temples, and impressive museums (Anagnost, 1997; McNeal, 2012). A strong historical sense of the ancient Chinese nation is conveyed both spatially and visually through various heritage projects. This phenomenon has been bolstered by the introduction of the global heritage discourse, particularly with the establishment of the World Heritage

Sites designation in 1972. China signed the UNESCO World Heritage Convention in 1985, and since 1987 has actively pursued the nomination of various historical sites as World Heritage candidates. Furthermore, the adoption of the Convention for the Safeguarding of Intangible Cultural Heritage in 2004 has further deepened China's commitment to preserving its traditional culture and practices.

Since China began its extensive economic and social transformation following reforms in 1978, there has been a notable resurgence of interest in the country's historical heritage. This interest reflects a desire to reconcile with past ideological shifts and the rapid societal changes brought about during the reform era. This appreciation of tradition and history marks a sharp contrast to Mao's era, when iconoclasm sought to erase China's historical legacy. The shift in China's view of its heritage emerged not only in response to the global heritage discourse but also within a specific political and social context. Beginning in the 1980s, as the Communist Party transitioned from Marxist-Maoist ideology to a market economy, the move challenged its political legitimacy rooted in communism (Guo, 2004). This "crisis of faith," triggered by Deng Xiaoping's Open-Door policy, sparked significant social upheaval. In response to these ideological changes, the Chinese government not only vigorously promoted national traditions to rejuvenate the nation's culture and spirit but also made the appreciation of China's historical past a central component of various political projects, even institutionalizing it. For example, Chinese state rhetoric has reinterpreted Confucianism in various political contexts. Political leaders such as Jiang Zemin publicly endorsed Confucian values, reasserting Chinese culture as Confucian and highlighting how patriotism and tradition harmonize with socialism (Guo, 2004, pp. 30, 74). Xi Jinping has rhetorically embraced the "China Dream (中國夢)," positioning China's rich traditions as sources of national pride and confidence. In 1994, a project was launched that framed heritage sites and museums as a basis for patriotism. The integration of historical narratives and traditional values into patriotic education underscores both China's millennia-old cultural glory and its more recent challenges, shaping the official narrative of China's global ascent (Callahan, 2005; Guo, 2004). "Cultural heritage" has been strategically employed to foster nationalism and provide a moral foundation for the legitimacy of the Chinese state as it transitioned from Marxist ideology to a reform-oriented era aimed at achieving a "spiritual socialist civilization" and a "harmonious society" (Madsen, 2014). This renewed embrace of China's historical past and traditional culture is being fueled by the nation's economic development and a surge in national confidence. This national revival mirrors global trends in heritage appreciation, where relics, traditional cultures, and historical narratives are increasingly valued as national or World Heritage sites, strengthening local and national pride and identity. As a result, the Chinese heritage landscape has become distinctly shaped by political instruments.

Additionally, since the 1980s, there has been a rise in "academic nationalism," with official sponsorship and extensive study of Chinese philosophies such as Confucianism and Daoism attracting more followers and enthusiasts (Guo, 2004, p. 124). At the local level, many Chinese intellectuals have actively advocated for using traditional Chinese values to guide society, sparking widespread enthusiasm known as the "national essence fever" (國學熱) across the country. Recent scholarship has observed a new trend over the past decade: the emergence of neotraditionalism and new Confucianism. This is evident in the global expansion of Confucius institutes and the revival of interest in traditional attire (known as the Hanfu revival movement), driven by grassroots individuals and local actors, that traces its origins to Huangdi as the progenitor of Chinese civilization and promotes a distinct vision of traditional clothing (Carrico, 2017). The cults of the Yellow Emperor and various other deified ancestors have emerged within a nationwide zeal for China's national past.

At the same time, indigenous popular religion, which has guided moral conduct in Chinese society for centuries, is undergoing a resurgence. This revival of popular religion has simultaneously fueled growth in religious tourism within China. As China opened up and underwent reforms, increased citizen mobility facilitated the rise of heritage tourism, exemplified by Han Chinese visiting destinations like Lijiang for ethnic tourism (Zhu, 2018). Oakes and Sutton (2010, pp. 6–7) note how government-managed tourism guides citizens toward exemplary modern behavior.

Madsen (2014), McNeal (2015), and Oakes and Sutton (2010) all emphasize the pivotal role of heritage in serving as a moral framework for regulating Chinese society. They note the resurgence of popular religion in China, reflected in the contemporary framing of heritage as a tool for patriotic education and cultural confidence. This includes the designation of temples, monuments, and cultural practices as heritage sites. This revival of China's historical consciousness can be attributed to the country's transition to a market economy, the rise of new Confucianism (which integrates Marxism with traditional culture to rejuvenate capitalism), and the promotion of a moral society with exemplary figures, all reflecting the state's efforts to nurture national identity.

Across the discussed heritage sites, markers of patriotic education are prominently displayed, promoting nationalism through heritage preservation. Scholars studying cultural heritage in China have found that heritage legitimizes political governance and contributes to social cohesion and stability. However, these analyses often overlook the roles played by various non-state entities in the heritage-making process and fail to recognize how heritage discourse can reshape or even promote new historical narratives, thereby reformulating regional identities. This Element finds that the appropriation of heritage discourse is playing a significant role in shaping regional and local identities in China. It will explore this further through case studies of the cults of the Yellow Emperor in various localities in China.

## Intangible Cultural Heritage in China

Since the 1980s, a significant influx of discourse on UNESCO's World Heritage has permeated China, igniting a distinctive heritage fever phenomenon. Nearly every year, a new potential heritage site has been nominated for World Cultural Heritage status, contributing to the largest number of designated heritage sites globally. The introduction of global heritage discourse has profoundly influenced Chinese society over the past forty years, notably reshaping the definition of "cultural heritage" through the formulation of new principles and revisions in cultural heritage laws (Wang & Rowlands, 2017). In 2001, Kunqu opera was designated as a Masterpiece of the Oral and Intangible Heritage of Humanity by UNESCO. Furthermore, the UNESCO Convention for the Safeguarding of the Intangible Cultural Heritage was adopted in 2003, and China ratified this international convention the following year, thereby introducing the concept of "intangible cultural heritage (Fei wuzhi wenhua yichan 非物質文化遺產)." According to the UNESCO convention, ICH includes five domains:

- oral traditions and expressions, including language as a vehicle of the ICH;
- performing arts;
- social practices, rituals, and festive events;
- knowledge and practices concerning nature and the universe;
- traditional craftsmanship.

The introduction of ICH into China has facilitated the revival of folk religions, traditions, and customs that were previously restricted, but are now rebranded and protected under the framework of "cultural heritage." In 2005, the Chinese government officially issued two documents: the *Opinions of the State Council General Office on Strengthening the Protection of China's Intangible Cultural Heritage* (State Council of the People's Republic of China, 2005b) and the *Notice of the State Council on Strengthening Cultural Heritage Protection* (State Council of the People's Republic of China, 2005a). These documents were aligned with UN conventions and marked the nationwide initiation of the application and evaluation process for "national-level" ICH projects. By July 2024, China had announced five batches of national-level ICH lists in 2006, 2008, 2011,

**Table 1** Number of entries in the five lists of ICH in China, updated through 2024

|  | 2006 (I) | 2008 (II) | 2011 (III) | 2014 (IV) | 2021 (V) |
|---|---|---|---|---|---|
| Folk literature | 53 | 79 | 58 | 40 | 21 |
| Traditional music | 100 | 208 | 44 | 49 | 30 |
| Traditional dance | 74 | 139 | 65 | 46 | 32 |
| Traditional opera | 181 | 161 | 77 | 26 | 28 |
| Narrative/storytelling traditions | 54 | 90 | 31 | 18 | 20 |
| Traditional sports, recreational activities, and acrobatics | 18 | 52 | 31 | 23 | 42 |
| Traditional arts | 77 | 182 | 46 | 54 | 58 |
| Traditional handicraft skills | 112 | 224 | 90 | 80 | 123 |
| Traditional medicine | 13 | 40 | 36 | 48 | 45 |
| Folk customs | 81 | 177 | 89 | 79 | 66 |
| Total | **763** | **1 352** | **567** | **463** | **465** |

**Source:** Compiled by the author based on information taken from China Intangible Cultural Heritage Network and China Intangible Cultural Heritage Digital Museum (2024b).

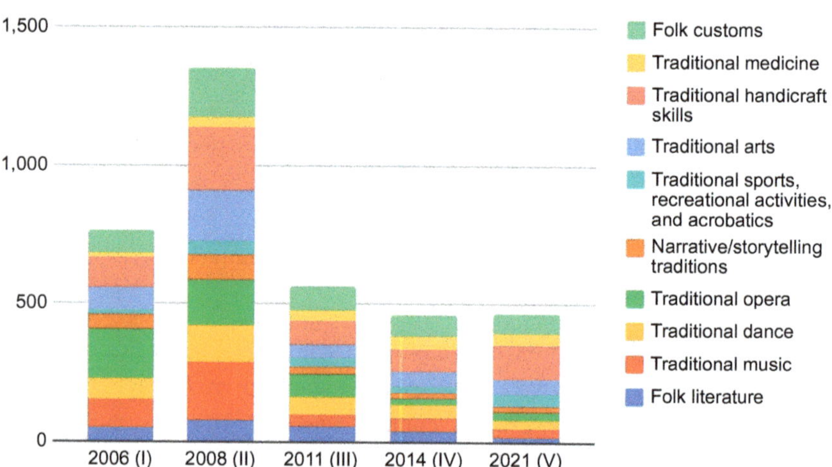


**Figure 1** Table of the five lists of ICH in China, updated through 2024.

**Source:** Compiled by the author based on information staken from China Intangible Cultural Heritage Network and China Intangible Cultural Heritage Digital Museum (2024b).

2014, and 2021, comprising a total of 3,610 items (Table 1, Figure 1). The concept of "heritage bearers (or inheritors) (*Fei wuzhi wenhua yichan chungchenren* 非物質文化遺產傳承人)" was introduced alongside ICH. By 2024, five batches –

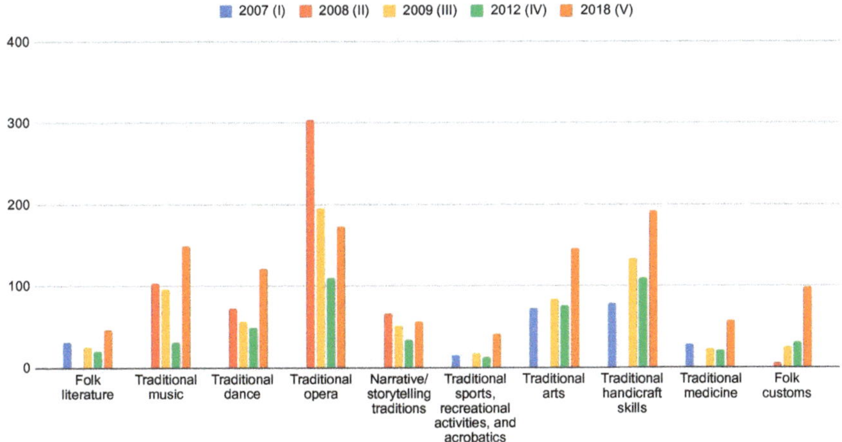



**Figure 2** Number of representative inheritors of national ICH in China, updated through 2024.

**Source:** Compiled by the author based on information taken from China Intangible Cultural Heritage Network and China Intangible Cultural Heritage Digital Museum (2024a).

selected in 2007, 2008, 2009, 2012, and 2018 – had been established, totaling 3,057 national heritage bearers (Figure 2). China employs four levels of protection and selection – national, provincial, city, and county – in the designation and safeguarding of ICH. The National List of Intangible Cultural Heritage is established through successive applications and evaluations based on provincial-level lists, ultimately receiving approval from the State Council, denoting its national significance. In 2011, the Law of the People's Republic of China on Intangible Cultural Heritage (2011) was passed, providing a more comprehensive legal framework for the protection of ICH.

Notably, within China's ICH categories there are ten items: folk customs; traditional medicine; traditional handicraft skills; traditional arts; traditional sports, recreational activities, and acrobatics; narrative/storytelling traditions; traditional opera; traditional dance; traditional music; and folk literature. Many elements of these, particularly those related to religious practices and ethnic traditions, which were once dismissed as superstitions in favor of modernity during the New Cultural Movement (1915) and the May Fourth Movement (1919), are now recognized as part of ICH. With the gradual political loosening following the 1978 opening-up, folklorists began to study folk beliefs more openly (Wu, 2009). However, during this period, the study of folk beliefs – incorporated into the broader folklore tradition – often concentrated on rites of passage, funerals, temple festivals, and material culture rather than on the "religions" themselves (Wu, 2009). As noted by Chen (2010), during the 1980s when the state launched the "Chinese Folk Literature Integration Project," local cultural practitioners faced uncertainties regarding the categorization of folk beliefs and religion under the religious policies of that era, posing challenges for researchers. It wasn't until the 2000s that this field truly flourished within the discourse of ICH, and folk beliefs have been allocated a specific place in national discussions through a series of national surveys of ICH (Chen, 2010; Gao, 2007; Wu, 2009). This inclusion of traditional festivals and folk rituals in the national lists of ICH under the "folk customs" section has sparked a new discourse in folklore studies regarding the relationship between folk beliefs and ICH. Within this new framework, religious practices are sometimes categorized under festivals such as temple fairs and traditional festivals, and at other times under narrative traditions, dance, or music.

In addition to the institutional framework, there were political motivations for promoting the revival of folk religions, particularly those that could strengthen national identity among the Chinese people and overseas Chinese communities. As described by Wu (2009) and Ku (2018), in the early 1980s, for example, with Mazu belief being one of the most popular religious practices and goddess figures in Taiwan, and following mainland China's opening to the world in 1978, many Taiwanese embarked on pilgrimages to Mazu's hometown in Fujian and to Mazu temples predominantly in southern China. This prompted the mainland Chinese government to emphasize and promote the study of Mazu. The revival of Mazu belief began, under the guise of "folk culture" or "folk belief," to replace "superstitions," with Mazu worship in Fujian becoming a symbol of "Fujian-Taiwan folk culture" in mainstream media discourse from 1983 onwards. The Mazu ceremony was nominated for inclusion on the first list of national intangible heritage in 2006, and later "Mazu belief" was recognized as UNESCO ICH in 2009, marking the first instance of a folk belief or religion from China to achieve such status. This recognition undoubtedly carries a significant political message.

Remote ancestral cults, which sought to identify a common ancestor for the Chinese people and to integrate them into a grand historical narrative of ancient Chinese history, were among the first to receive official recognition within the new framework of ICH. For example, the first list, compiled in 2006 with seventy items, includes eleven related to religious practices, mostly focusing on common ancestral cults such as the Huangdi, Yandi, Dayu, Fuxi, Nüwa, Confucius, and Genghis Khan. After the first designation, in the 2006 *Handbook for the Survey of Intangible Cultural Heritage in China* by the China Arts Center, folk religious practices are listed among sixteen items included in ICH (Chen, 2010). This handbook serves as the basis for ICH designation across cultural departments nationwide. Viewing folk beliefs through the lens of ICH enables complementary research into the rituals and customs associated with these beliefs, thereby highlighting their cultural significance and reinforcing their legitimacy (Wu, 2009). It is through this step-by-step process of study and designation that the Chinese state openly acknowledges folk beliefs as part of ICH.

## Religious Revivals in China

Since the early twentieth century, the question of how to define "religion" in state discourse has been contentious. Chinese folk religions, known as *Minjian Xinyang* (民間信仰), are referred to by various English terms such as religion, folk beliefs, popular cult, popular religion, and communal religion (Chen, 2010).[1] They incorporate sources from Confucianism, Buddhism, Taoism, and Legalism traditions. During the Republican era (1911~1949 in mainland China), folk religious practices and Confucian ideology were viewed as hindrances to progress and modernity. Even in the late Qing period, many Taoist, Buddhist, and Confucian temples were converted into public or private schools as part of reform efforts to adopt Western knowledge and science. In 1949, with the establishment of the People's Republic of China, the Chinese Communist Party, as atheists, attempted to outlaw religious beliefs, viewing all religious activities, including ancestral worship, as feudal superstitions. Temples and ritual practices were especially targeted during the Cultural Revolution (1966–1976), when all public religious activities were banned.

However, since the reform era, ancestral worship and folk temples in China have seen a resurgence and signs of prosperity. The revival of folk religious activities began during this period, initially driven by grassroots initiatives, as ordinary people started to revive ancestral worship and temple beliefs (Chau, 2006; Gao, 2004). These activities were often categorized as tourist festivals or temple fairs, as "religion" continues to be heavily censored by the central state and the bureau of religions. During the 1990s, amid the trend of "culture as the stage, economy as the performance" across diverse regions, local governments increasingly embraced the integration of folk belief activities into temple fairs and cultural tourism initiatives. This strategic approach facilitated the resurgence of traditional practices, including rural temple festivals and other forms of beliefs.

---

[1] These terms refer to different meanings and practices, varying by temporal and regional contexts. Since each requires detailed scholarly analysis, their definitions are not the focus of this Element.

In China, as described by Wu (2009), the construction of temples follows a standard procedure. Initially, it requires approval from the religious authorities, followed by the issuance of a land use certificate from the land management bureau, and approval of the design plans by the construction planning department. In the 1990s, the various levels of religious administration departments had sufficient policy reasons to reject applications for land use certificates for temple construction plans related to folk beliefs (Wu, 2009). However, when local governments develop cultural tourism, they often establish temples within museums, memorial halls, tourist attractions, and parks, all managed under the bureaus of culture or tourism, in the name of promoting cultural tourism. Therefore, when applying for land use, they cleverly circumvent the management regulations of religious institutions and other departments, directly using the identity of cultural institutions to construct a legal cultural rationale for themselves (Wu, 2009). Due to temples being designated as tourist attractions and charging high entrance fees, only visitors who purchase tickets can enter. This has led to criticism that religions are being used as a stage for tourism performances.

Gao (2004) has revealed how the "Dragon Brand Association (龍牌會)" in Hebei built up a "temple" in the name of a "museum" under the efforts of folk traditional belief organizations, scholars, and local literati to achieve the legitimate acquisition of folk temples. Through the study of the Black Dragon King Temple in northern China, Adam Chau (2006) explores the interaction patterns between local temples and local governments, including how grassroots religious revivals involve villagers in reviving religious practices and building local temples, as well as the adjustments and controls exerted by local governments. In his book *The Temple of Memories: History, Power, and Morality in a Chinese Village* (1996), Jing explores the reconstruction of an ancestral hall in Dachuan (大川), Gansu (甘肅) Province, focusing on its transformation into a Confucius Temple and examining the difficulties and strategies employed by villagers during the rebuilding process.

While local communities revived folk temples and their associated customs from a bottom-up surge, local governments incorporated them into their cultural and economic development, primarily through tourism. On a broader level, the central state, prior to the 2000s, did not actively interfere or enforce strict regulations, perhaps recognizing the role that folk religion could play in moral regulation (Madsen, 2014). These spontaneous revivals of folk religion have provided significant spiritual solace to the people during the transition from communist political ideology to the Reform and Opening-Up period. Jing (1996) examines how memory, power, and moral authority within the village were reflected in the temple rebuilding project between the 1980s and the 1990s, showing how historical narratives and local identities evolve and interact over time. Jing (1996) reveals how Dachuan villagers use "memory" to rebuild social relationships and adapt to challenges, impacting the revival of folk religion and the restructuring of rituals. For example, a key innovation in the reconstruction of the ancestral hall was the creation of a new Confucius Temple, which expanded ancestor worship – initially reserved for the Kong descendants from Dachuan (大川) – to include all villagers in 22 nearby villages (about 20,000 people). In the process of creating Confucius statues, the Kong family unintentionally transformed their ancestor into a non-ancestral deity. By identifying as descendants of Confucius, they turned the exclusive practice of ancestor worship into an inclusive Confucian ritual for the entire village. This effort was driven by a growing sense of identity, spontaneous social groups, and community self-governance, highlighting how such efforts shape local identity. Madsen's fieldwork in temples across Handan and Wenzhou illustrates the revitalization of folk religious practices and ancestral shrines, which serve as moral touchstones for societal norms. Similarly, studies by McNeal (2012, 2015) document the commemoration of figures like Sage King Shun and the promotion of ancestor worship in regions like Wuhan and Hebei Province. Local elites have invested in constructing temples and monuments dedicated to these figures, aiming to bolster local identity and stimulate the regional economy.

It was not until UNESCO's ICH convention was recognized by Chinese officials in 2003 that these religious activities were officially permitted and integrated into cultural heritage projects across China. With the inclusion of traditional festivals and folk rituals in the "folk customs" section of the national ICH list, the relationship between folk beliefs and ICH has emerged as a new discourse in folklore studies. The recognition of ICH by authorities has led to the revival of traditional practices once considered feudal superstitions, elevating them to the status of cultural heritage. Once an advocate of Marxist ideology and viewing heritage as an obstacle to modernity, China now proudly celebrates its 5,000-year cultural heritage, and religion is not only surviving but flourishing (Johnson, 2017; Madsen, 2014). Despite having the largest population of non-religious individuals and a government that espouses atheism, religious practices continue to thrive. Yet not all traditions and religions are recognized; it is only through obtaining ICH status that they gain official recognition, enhancing China's global image and influence and portraying the nation as culturally continuous. Otherwise, they continue to be dismissed as superstitions. Chinese scholars have noted that approaching the study of folk beliefs from the perspective of ICH grants them a rightful place in public discourse, which is essential for their presentation. Wu (2009) argued that this approach could legitimize the intangible aspects of folk beliefs. However, Gao (2007) critically observed that when folk beliefs are acknowledged as "intangible heritage," it further solidifies their identity as "folk culture" and "customary culture," positioning them as relics of historical traditions and pillars of ethnic memory.

With the resurgence of folk religion during the Reform and Opening-Up period, ancestor worship was the first to experience a revival, and remote ancestral cults were the most widely recognized officially. These ancestral cults, which had been in decline for a century, are helping to foster a sense of pride in lineage and tradition linking individuals to a larger shared historical narrative. Each year, tens of thousands of Chinese return to their hometowns to participate in ancestor worship activities. Despite previous restrictions on many religious practices, the Qingming Festival has been established as a national holiday and recognized as a national-level ICH. As a result, central and local governments, as well as various clans and organizations both within China and abroad, have been allowed and even encouraged to carry out ancestor worship activities.

Belief in the "Yellow Emperor," for example, which this Element examines, began to resurge in various regions during the 1990s on a relatively localized level. Official recognition of the Yellow Emperor as a common ancestor of the Chinese people began after 2000, with ceremonies gradually established in Shaanxi, Henan, Zhejiang, and other areas under the leadership of provincial governments. The Yellow Emperor ceremonies in Henan, Shaanxi, and Zhejiang were designated as national-level ICH in 2006, 2008, and 2011, respectively. According to legend, the Yellow Emperor is viewed as the common ancestor of the Chinese nation and the creator of Chinese culture. As belief in the Yellow Emperor revived, regions began competing to host national-level worship ceremonies. For instance, Henan Province claims to be the birthplace of the Yellow Emperor and thus asserts exclusive rights to "Huangdi culture." In contrast, Shaanxi Province emphasizes that the Yellow Emperor was buried there and that official ceremonies have been held since the Tang Dynasty, thus claiming its own authority over "Huangdi culture." Many other regions use historical records, oral histories, or relics from Huangdi temples to claim their connections to the Yellow Emperor. In fact, there are even competitions among various localities within Henan Province to assert their association with Huangdi culture. Today, the intense competition between regions such as Shaanxi and Henan to host a national-level ceremony and assert control over Huangdi culture highlights the distinctive nature of cultural heritage discourse in China. Beyond this competition, since 2003, numerous localities across China have organized large-scale remote ancestral ceremonies.

Additionally, even party officials are encouraged to visit the sites of remote ancestors as part of their annual training in communism. During my fieldwork in

China in 2023, I observed that, aside from the dates of grand ceremonies, individuals, businesses, and government officials – who, as Communist Party members, are typically expected to adhere to atheism – participate in organized group trips to these sites. These visits allow these officials to learn about Chinese history and pay respects to their ancestors as part of their patriotic education. This approach is endorsed by the government as part of its promotion of sites of patriotic education.

Yet these religious revivals are selective, a trend that became particularly evident following the promotion of religious Sinicization (Zhongjia zhongguohua 宗教中國化) in 2012, which was officially endorsed by Xi Jinping in 2015 (Y. Wang, 2021; Xinhua News Agency, 2021). There is a noticeable trend of Sinicization of religions, where the religious groups are required to operate under the state's sanction and to incorporate patriotic education (Y. Wang, 2021). In 2018, the Religious Affairs Regulations came into effect, leading to the removal of Catholic crosses and the renovation of mosque buildings. Five approved national religious organizations – Buddhism, Taoism, Islam, Catholicism, and Protestantism – are required to operate within their sanctioned frameworks under the supervision of the National Religious Affairs Administration. State-sanctioned Catholic and Christian churches have been rebranded as "Patriotic Churches" under government oversight. Unregistered religious groups face varying degrees of harassment and destruction. Among the five officially recognized religions in China, there is evident repression of institutionalized religions from "abroad" such as Islam, Catholicism, and Protestantism. Examples include the demolition of Christian churches in Zhejiang in 2016 and Henan in 2018, and nationwide crackdowns on Catholicism (Y. Wang, 2021). In contrast, indigenous religions like Taoism and Buddhism have been successfully integrated into the Chinese government's religious framework as they contribute to the broader discourse of fostering nationalism and pride in history and heritage. Within this trend, under the banners of nationalism and patriotism, indigenous religious practices, particularly remote ancestral cults that venerate China's historical past and strengthen national unity, enjoy broad support compared to other religious practices. These practices are conducted by various levels of local governments.

In summary, religion in contemporary China is being selectively revived, focusing primarily on indigenous religions such as folk beliefs, especially those recognized as ICH. The evolution of these beliefs – from being initially classified as "superstition" to being acknowledged as "folk culture," and now as part of the expanding concept of "ICH" – represents a significant transformation in the perception and revival of *Minjian xinyang*.

## Internalized Heritage Discourse in China

Thanks to UNESCO's World Heritage discourse, localities in China are engaged in competitive efforts to establish themselves as the hometowns of "historical figures" by designating sites as heritage. Regional and local governments are striving to register cultural expressions associated with these historical celebrities for intangible heritage status, starting at regional levels and progressing to national and global recognition. Such cultural expressions encompass rituals, dances, music, and oral histories. In recent years, a new cultural form known as "grand ceremony" has emerged. Crucially, these ceremonies are modern inventions that blend historical traditions with contemporary expressions.

Studies have demonstrated that the designation of World Heritage items can enhance national pride and identity (Yan, 2018), promote tourism and economic development (Zhu & Maags, 2020), and cultivate new forms of heritage consumption (Zhu, 2018). However, despite these comprehensive studies on heritage in China, there remains a gap in explaining why the Chinese state is more assertive in designating cultural heritage compared to other nations, as well as the intense competition among Chinese localities for these designations. My research reveals a distinct internalization of heritage discourse within China. While the central government ambitiously participates in the global heritage arena by nominating World Heritage Sites, adhering to international conventions, and redefining the legal definition of heritage according to global standards, localities within China are utilizing heritage designations domestically to redefine themselves. Political scientists have analyzed how gross domestic product (GDP) targets foster competitive regionalism. I argue that this competition also manifests in the cultural realm, particularly in the formal recognition of heritage sites. In this Element I explore how local competition shapes the construction of heritage and transforms religious practices, ultimately contributing to the development of new historical narratives that support regional identities.

Since the revival of ancestor worship and the discourse on UNESCO heritage after the Reform and Opening-Up period, the worship of the Yellow Emperor has become widely revitalized since the 2000s. Interestingly, today, various provinces in China are vying for ownership of "Huangdi culture" as if it were a possessable entity. In 2005, the government of Shaanxi Province designated the Yellow Emperor's ceremonies held within the province as provincial-level ICH, and included them in the national-level ICH the following year. Similarly, ceremonies honoring ancestors organized by Henan Province in Xinzheng City have been led on a large scale by the provincial government since 2006, and were recognized by the State Council as national-level ICH in 2008. Jinyun's Yellow Emperor ceremony in Zhejiang Province was recognized as national-level ICH in 2011. All three provinces claim legitimacy in their worship of the Yellow Emperor. Other areas, such as Zhuolu in Hebei Province, Zhengning (正寧) in Gansu Province, and Qufu (曲阜) in Shandong (山東), are also vying for ownership of Huangdi culture. As Sangren (2000, p. 16) noted, "history becomes a heavily ideologically inflected discourse complexly embedded in the sometimes congenial and sometimes strained relations between localities and the state."

## Rivalry among Localities

As part of the revival of ancestor worship and folk religion in Reform Era China (1978–), the 1990s saw a resurgence in popular religion, including the localized worship of Huangdi in various places. Since the 2000s, there has been a growing trend for localities to connect their regions with remote ancestors, revered deities, and/or famous historical figures. For example, Henan's Zhoukou Huaiyang (周口淮揚) and Gansu's Tianshui (天水) both claim the legacy of the remote ancestor Fuxi. Similarly, Shanxi's Linfen (山西臨汾), Hebei's Handan Shexian (邯鄲涉縣), and Gansu's Qinan (秦安) compete over the legacy of the remote ancestor Nüwa. Hunan's Zhuzhou Yanling (湖南株洲炎陵), Shanxi's Gaoping (高平), Shaanxi's Baoji (寶雞), and Henan's Shanqiu (商丘) vie for the heritage of Emperor Yan. Hunan's Ningyuan (寧遠) and Shanxi's Yuncheng (運城) contest over Emperor Shun, while Henan's Luyi (鹿邑) and Anhui's Woyang (安徽渦陽) compete for the title of Laoyi's hometown, to name just a few. Even for historical figures like Zhuge Liang (諸葛亮), there are competing claims to his legacy. Shandong's Linyi (臨沂) asserts itself as his birthplace, while Henan's Nanyang (南陽) and Hubei's Xiangyang (襄陽) vie for recognition as his established residence. Furthermore, Shaanxi's Hanzhong (漢中) claims to be his burial site. Despite these distinctions, all these locations vie for the right to honor and assert ownership of this historical figure's legacy. These places all compete with each other, claiming exclusive rights to the cultural heritage associated with their locations, and the governments organize large-scale ceremonies to honor these ancestors. Additionally, they are applying for ICH designations for customs, festivals, and legends (oral histories) related to these figures at various levels.

Despite the extensive historical sources and legends about Huangdi, as well as the numerous temples dedicated to him across China, several localities are now competing for ownership of "Huangdi culture," treating it as a brand to be possessed. Each region uses different historical sources to justify its exclusive claim to Huangdi culture. For instance, Xinzheng in Henan cites the "Bamboo

Annals (竹書紀年)" as evidence of the Yellow Emperor's hometown, while Qufu in Shandong refers to the "Records of the Grand Historian (史記)." The competition extends to claims about the Yellow Emperor's burial site. Huangling County in Shaanxi points to the "Records of the Grand Historian: Basic Annals of the Five Emperors," which states: "The Yellow Emperor passed away and was buried at Mount Qiao." Zhengning County in Gansu also cites this record but claims that Mount Qiao within Gansu is the true burial site. Zhuolu County in Hebei asserts that it was the location of the Yellow Emperor's battle against Chiyou and cites the "Commentary on the Water Classic (水經注)" to suggest that Zhuolu has historically been a site of Huangdi worship. This competition for legitimacy is widespread among contemporary provinces such as Xinzheng, Qufu, Huangling, Zhuolu, Zhengning, and Jinyun, all of which host official ceremonies honoring the Yellow Emperor and feature statues recognized as part of ICH. In this context, various regions of contemporary China are engaged in a fierce competition using their respective historical documents to lay claim to the legacy of the Yellow Emperor. They not only compete for the legacy of the Yellow Emperor's existence in various provinces but also contest the legitimacy of their places as the traditional sites for worshipping the Yellow Emperor over dynasties.

In this Element I argue for an internalization of heritage discourse in China, where localities brand themselves with heritage status. It is evident that localities are competing to brand themselves through promoting various ancestral cults and by designating heritage statues. I further present how contemporary China is undergoing extensive placemaking processes alongside the heritagization processes (Wang, 2016). These places have all undergone large-scale placemaking, including the creation of large parks, the erection of monuments, and the establishment of temples and museums. In China, placemaking is marked by a fervent desire to brand localities with heritage labels, mirroring UNESCO heritage initiatives aimed at culturally branding locations. As part of attaining heritage status, places are defined by their distinctive "culture (文化 *wenhua*)." I argue that, in China, localities act as collective entities, treating cultural heritage as proprietary and utilizing it to define themselves, thereby asserting ownership over designated heritage "culture" (e.g., Handler, 1988). This Element illustrates how cultural heritage functions as a "name card (名片 *mingpian*)," strategically used by localities to distinguish themselves. Moreover, official cultural heritage status is employed to authenticate historical narratives as localities cultivate their local and regional consciousness through heritage-making, effectively reshaping history.

## 3 The Search for a Common Ancestor

### The Search for a National Past

In the late nineteenth century, the establishment of nation-states in Europe heightened people's demands for allegiance, and, as a result, collective memory became a catalyst for national fervor (Olick, 2007). Koselleck (1985) illustrated that during the eighteenth and nineteenth centuries, Europe saw the emergence of a new historical consciousness, characterized by what he termed "collective singularity." This shift in historical consciousness moved beyond isolated events to encompass broader historical periods (*Geschichte*), and from a retrospective focus on the past to a prospective consideration of the future. Individual historical narratives gradually coalesced into a collective understanding, fostering an imagined history. Furthermore, Gadamer (1994) introduced the concept of "historically affected consciousness," suggesting that individuals are influenced by the historical and cultural contexts that have shaped them, whether or not they are consciously aware of these influences.

In a similar vein, in the late nineteenth and early twentieth centuries, China underwent a transformation from an imperial system to a modern nation-state, which brought forth a new perspective on its past. Intellectuals grappled with questions about the essence of China's historical legacy and how to construct a national history suitable for the modern era. Concurrently, there was a surge of public interest in Chinese autochthonous ancestors. Liu (2019) contends that this transition propelled traditional historiography toward modern methods, marking a significant shift in how history was written. It wasn't until the early twentieth century that scholars endeavored to formulate China's first chronological calendar, marking a pivotal moment in the formalization of Chinese historical chronology.[2]

This process echoes Benedict Anderson's (1983) concept of *imagined communities*, which emphasizes the role of print capitalism in the formation of modern nations. Anderson argues that print media – particularly the spread of newspapers, books, and other forms of mass communication – played a crucial role in standardizing language, creating a shared sense of belonging, and fostering national identity. In the late nineteenth and early twentieth centuries, it was recognized that there was a need for a unified national narrative, to enable nation building; this prompted historians and archaeologists from the twentieth

---

[2] China has long been proud of its rich tradition of historical writing. In imperial times, each dynasty documented the history of its predecessor to legitimize royal genealogies. However, these narratives were primarily focused on political events and the accounts of royal dynastic families, with no concept of writing a comprehensive national history.

century onward to delve into the origins of Chinese civilization. This quest aimed to establish a linear historical trajectory, delineate national ethnicities, and demarcate national boundaries. Over time, diverse individual histories and regional narratives amalgamated into a cohesive national timeline, as described by Duara (1995). He argues that national history constructs a semblance of unity for nations embroiled in complexity and uncertainty, presenting a consistent national subject evolving through time.

At this pivotal moment of political and social transformation, beginning in the late nineteenth and early twentieth centuries, there was a notable surge in public enthusiasm for Huangdi, the Yellow Emperor. But who exactly was Huangdi? As a legendary figure from antiquity, Huangdi is surrounded by multiple origin stories and associations. One prominent narrative holds that approximately 4,000 to 5,000 years ago, Huangdi founded the first Chinese nation by triumphing over the evil king Chiyou and his counterpart Yandi (Liu, 1999). Revered as the foremost leader among ancient sages, Huangdi is credited with pioneering agriculture, establishing the lunar calendar system, advancing medicine, and developing techniques in weaving, pottery, clothing, housing, and currency – attributes that earned him the title of the founding father of Chinese civilization.

## The Yellow Emperor in Historical Narratives

In his works, Michael Herzfeld (1991, 1997) argues that history is not remembered and represented neutrally or objectively but is shaped by social, political, and cultural forces. Using Greece as a case study, he explores how societies "imagine" history, shaping the past to serve contemporary needs. Herzfeld contends that historical imagination is a dynamic, selective process influenced by power, social context, and cultural practices. He emphasizes that historical narratives are actively constructed, not passive reflections of past events, and play a crucial role in shaping collective identity, memory, and political power. Herzfeld highlights how individuals and communities use historical memory to navigate contemporary life and construct national identities.

Similarly, the historical narratives surrounding the Yellow Emperor, both in ancient Chinese texts and today, reveal how his portrayal has evolved over time. The discourse surrounding him traces back to the ninth century and has since reached a new peak, taking on a contemporary form in the present day. His position within China's "Five Emperors" and "Three Sovereigns" has also shifted multiple times throughout history. Chinese popular discourse holds that the Yellow Emperor is considered the common ancestor of the Chinese people and the founder of Chinese culture. However, records about the Yellow

Emperor only appeared during the Spring and Autumn and the Warring States periods (770–221 BC). Records of "ancestors" in pre-Spring and Autumn works like "The Book of History (尚書)" and "The Book of Odes and Hymns (詩經)" trace back at most to sage Yu (禹) and Houji (后稷) (Sun, 2000, p. 69). Western Zhou (1046–770 BC) inscriptions trace ancestors no further back than King Wen (文王) and King Wu (武王). The Yellow Emperor only began to be widely mentioned in documents from the Warring States (475/403–221 BC) to the early Han Dynasty (202 BC–AD 220). Initially, he was listed alongside ancient emperors such as Fuxi, Gonggong (共工), and Shennong (神農). It wasn't until the first century BC that the Han historian Sima Qian, in the "Records of the Grand Historian," established him as the first ancestor among the Five Emperors of the Xia, Shang, and Zhou dynasties.

The portrayal of Huangdi (the Yellow Emperor) in ancient Chinese texts has undergone significant transformations, and the sequence and the identification of the Three Sovereigns and Five Emperors as common ancestors of the Chinese people have also changed over time. During this period, systematic theories about the Five Emperors emerged from works such as the "Annals of Lü Buwei (呂氏春秋)" and "The Master of Huainan (淮南子)." The Five Emperors mentioned are Taihao (太皞), the Yan Emperor, the Yellow Emperor, Shaohao (少皞), and Zhuanxu (顓頊). Sima Qian's "Records of the Grand Historian" lists the Five Emperors as the Yellow Emperor, Emperor Zhuanxu, Emperor Ku, Emperor Yao, and Emperor Shun. The "Greater Rites of the Han Dynasty: The Virtues of the Five Emperors (大戴禮記)" also adopts the theory of the Yellow Emperor, Emperor Zhuanxu, Emperor Ku, Emperor Yao, and Emperor Shun as the Five Emperors.

The name "Three Sovereigns" first appeared in the "Annals of Lü Buwei." The "Records of the Grand Historian: Annals of Emperor Qinshihuang" states that after Emperor Qinshihuang annexed various states, his ministers suggested that Qinshihuang's achievements surpassed those of the Five Emperors, unprecedented since ancient times, making him Grand Sovereign. In the Han Dynasty, the apocryphal texts "Spring and Autumn Annals (春秋緯)" and "Sequence of Fate (命歷序)" made the Three Sovereigns the Heavenly Sovereign (天皇), the Earthly Sovereign (地皇), and the Human Sovereign (人皇). Later, Han Confucians gradually abandoned the titles of Heavenly Sovereign, Earthly Sovereign, Grand Sovereign, and Human Sovereign, pairing the "Three Sovereigns" with ancient emperors. Most theories included Fuxi and Shennong, with the third being Nüwa, Suiren (燧人), Zhu Rong (祝融), or Gonggong. As for the "Records of the Grand Historian: Annals of the Three Sovereigns," it was supplemented by Sima Zhen (司法貞) of the Tang Dynasty (AD 618–907) describing the Three Sovereigns as Fuxi, Nüwa, and Shennong.

According to the "Records of the Grand Historian" annotations by Tang Dynasty scholar Huangfu Mi, "Fuxi, Shennong, and the Yellow Emperor were the Three Sovereigns," while the Five Emperors were Shaohao, Zhuanxu, Ku, Yao, and Shun (the Yellow Emperor became one of the Three Sovereigns, and Shaohao joined the Five Emperors). Yuan Dynasty temples of the Three Sovereigns also adopted this theory, establishing Fuxi, Shennong, and the Yellow Emperor as the Three Sovereigns.

The evolution of Huangdi's image from a historical to a legendary and mythological figure illustrates the dynamic nature of historical narrative construction. Initially, Huangdi appears sporadically in texts from the Warring States period, gaining prominence during the early Han Dynasty through the works of historians like Sima Qian. Sima Qian's "Records of the Grand Historian" formalized Huangdi as a central ancestral figure, integrating him into the genealogical framework of the Xia, Shang, and Zhou dynasties. The concept of the Three Sovereigns and Five Emperors also shifted over time, with various texts and scholars proposing different configurations. In works like "Annals of Lü Buwei" and "The Master of Huainan," the Five Emperors include Taihao, the Yan Emperor, the Yellow Emperor, Shaohao, and Zhuanxu, each associated with different elements and seasons. Sima Qian's list of Five Emperors – Huangdi, Zhuanxu, Ku, Yao, and Shun – became widely accepted. The Three Sovereigns, initially mentioned in "Annals of Lü Buwei" included figures such as Fuxi, Nüwa, and Shennong. During the Tang Dynasty, Sima Zhen's supplementation of "Records of the Grand Historian" further elaborated on these figures, incorporating them into a cohesive historical narrative.

By the late Qing period, the study of Huangdi and the broader mytho-historical framework had peaked, with global sinologists examining and debating his origins. During this time, many Chinese intellectuals worked on developing history as a modern discipline, distinguishing it from "myth (神話)," a concept introduced from Japan in the early twentieth century. This distinction between myth and history introduces a new temporal understanding of remote "history." Influenced by Western scientific and critical approaches, scholars like Gu Jiegang (顧頡剛), Ch'ien Mu (錢穆), and Hu Shi (胡適) critically examined the authenticity of Chinese historical records, often dismissing early history as mere mythology. Known as the "School of Doubting Antiquity (疑古學派)," this group critically examined and questioned the authenticity of ancient Chinese historical texts and traditions. They argued that many ancient texts were mythologized or written long after the events they described, casting doubt on their reliability. Gu Jiegang, a leading figure in this movement, encouraged a scientific perspective on ancient texts and figures. He questioned whether Huangdi was a historical figure mythologized over time or a mythological ancestor humanized and historicized. This movement gained prominence in the early Republican period (1912–1949) and continues to exert influence today. It encouraged a more critical and analytical approach to history, moving away from the uncritical acceptance of traditional narratives. However, it faced controversy, with some scholars and traditionalists criticizing it for undermining Chinese cultural heritage and national identity. The debate between traditionalists and skeptics continues to shape Chinese historiography. This ongoing challenge in Chinese historiography involves differentiating between myth and history and determining which sources to trust.

On the other hand, the late Qing and early Republican eras were periods of significant transition, marking the shift from imperial China to the establishment of a modern nation-state. During this time, there was a growing need to define national ethnicity and establish a continuous national history. Although the Chinese imperial project had long distinguished between the "civilized" Han people and "barbarians" (Dikotter, 1992), Western ideas of race and ethnicity were introduced to China in the late nineteenth century (Yang, 2010). This led Chinese intellectuals to reassess Chinese ethnicity.[3] For example, late Qing intellectual Liang Qichao (梁啟超) identified the Chinese people as the "Yellow race" (黃種) after learning that Europeans used the color yellow to symbolize China. This symbolism popularized terms like the Yellow River, Yellow land, Yellow race, and Yellow Emperor to refer China (Yang, 2010).

A significant development in the historiography of ancient China occurred with the establishment of the Yellow Emperor Era chronology by Liu Shipei (劉師培) in 1903. Liu, a late Qing intellectual, dated Huangdi's birth to 2711 BC in the Gregorian calendar (Cohen, 2012, p. 4). This chronology aimed to systematize the origins and evolution of the Han race and Han culture, linking historical events to specific dates and reinforcing a sense of continuity in Chinese civilization. Liu's work sought to reclaim and redefine Chinese identity amid modernization and foreign influence, positioning Huangdi within a historical timeline and emphasizing the deep roots of Han culture. This dating is one of several speculative dates for Huangdi's era, reflecting ongoing efforts to align myth with history. Liu's chronology is significant not only for dating Huangdi's birth but also for constructing a cohesive narrative of Han origins, focusing on kin relationships and cultural development.

This evolution reflects the complex interplay between myth, legend, and historical record in the construction of cultural and national identity. This

---

[3] Opinions varied on who should rightfully be designated as the ancestor of China, reflecting differing views on Chinese ethnicity. During the Republican era, scholars proposed that China comprised five ethnic groups: Han, Man, Mong, Hui, and Zang. However, since the establishment of the People's Republic of China in the 1950s, a nationwide ethnic identification project has recognized fifty-six ethnic groups within the Chinese nation (Fei, 1989).

ongoing scholarly discourse reflects the complexities of distinguishing history from myth in the construction of cultural heritage and identity. The narrative of Huangdi exemplifies how ancient figures can be reshaped to meet the evolving needs of historical memory and cultural symbolism.

## Official Worship of the Yellow Emperor in Imperial Times

Throughout imperial China, sacrificial ceremonies of the Yellow Emperor were divided into official worship (公祭) and private worship (民祭). Official worship refers to state-sponsored sacrificial ceremonies organized by the government or official institutions to honor ancestors, deities, or significant historical figures. These public sacrifices are often attended by officials, involving elaborate rituals, music, dance, and other ceremonial elements. They are conducted on a large scale and reflect the collective reverence of the state or community. Examples include state ceremonies held to honor the Yellow Emperor, Confucius, and other important cultural and historical figures. For example, in imperial times, the official worship of Confucius was a highly formalized and significant state ritual known as the "Confucius Worship Ceremony" or "Sacrificial Rites to Confucius" (祭孔大典). This ceremony was an important part of the state rituals and was conducted with great reverence and precision. The main ceremony took place at the Confucius Temple in Qufu, Shandong Province, Confucius' birthplace, or at the capital where the emperor, as the main host, presided over the ceremony alongside the Minister of Rites. Similar ceremonies were held at Confucius temples across China, conducted by various levels of administrative officials (Huang, 2015).

Ritual offerings included sacrificial animals (such as oxen, sheep, and pigs), wine, grains, silk, and other items. These offerings were presented on an altar before the spirit tablets of Confucius and his notable disciples. The ceremony featured ancient ritual music and elaborate dances known as the Six Rows Dance, performed by dancers in traditional attire. The music was played on classical instruments such as bells, chimes, and flutes.

Incense was burned, and prayers were recited to honor Confucius and seek blessings for the state, its people, and the cultivation of moral virtues. Passages from Confucian classics, such as the "Analects (論語)" and other important works, were recited as part of the ritual to underscore the importance of Confucian teachings. The ceremony was rich in symbolism, reflecting the core values of Confucianism such as respect for hierarchy and the importance of education, moral integrity, and social harmony. The emperor's participation signified the state's endorsement and promotion of Confucian values as the guiding principles of governance and society. The official worship of Confucius in imperial times was not just a religious or cultural event but also a political statement, reinforcing Confucian ideology as the foundation of the Chinese state and its governance.

When the emperor served as the host, it represented the highest level of official worship. From the Han Dynasty to the end of the Qing Dynasty, the state's official worship of the Yellow Emperor began to become standardized, with only minor details changing across different dynasties. Generally, there are three main aspects: (1) the Yellow Emperor was included in the grand rites of sacrificing to heaven and Earth as one of the celestial deities; (2) the Yellow Emperor was honored in the imperial temples dedicated to successive emperors, as one of the revered imperial figures; and (3) the Yellow Emperor's mausoleum was venerated as one of the royal tombs.

According to Liao (2016, pp. 513–514), Emperor Xiaowen (孝文帝) (AD 467–499) of the Northern Wei Dynasty was a key initiator in the state's official veneration of previous sovereigns and sages, and became the origin of state rituals for earlier emperors from the Sui and Tang dynasties onward. During the reign of Emperor Xiaowen of the Northern Wei to Emperor Xuanzong (宣宗) of the Tang Dynasty, it was found that not only did the rituals become increasingly stable but the continuity of worship of the Three Sovereigns and Five Emperors was also highlighted through the inclusion of Emperor Ku in the state sacrificial rites. Liao also emphasizes that the changes and re-confirmations of sacrificial locations are crucial in distinguishing official rites from popular folk altars. However, how these locations were decided remains a question. Liao (2016, p. 538) argues that Emperor Xiaowen's decisions regarding sacrificial sites and subsequent changes were not based on old or singular criteria but were the result of a balance achieved by inheriting existing traditions and reconciling different theories. Liao's research has illustrated how the Yellow Emperor has had different representations throughout history, and the Three Sovereigns and Five Emperors as the ancestors of the Chinese nation have been referred to differently over time. Temples and tombs established for official and private worship during imperial times have become key sites for today's grand ceremonies, which are often held competitively to assert their legitimacy.

Private worship refers to informal sacrificial ceremonies performed by individuals, families, or local communities. These private sacrifices are typically smaller in scale and may involve personal or family rites conducted at home, in ancestral halls, or at local temples. These ceremonies are deeply rooted in local customs and traditions and reflect the personal piety and cultural heritage of the participants. Examples include family ancestor worship during festivals such as Qingming Festival, Double Ninth Festival, or personal offerings at local shrines. Both official and private acts of worship illustrate the structured and regulated nature of ritual practice in imperial China, balancing the need for reverent observance with practical considerations that could necessitate temporary exemptions.

## The Yellow Emperor in Popular Religious Discourse

As observed by many anthropologists studying China, the elevation of notable individuals into lineage genealogies (e.g., Faure, 2007; Siu, 1990) and their subsequent worship as deities (e.g., Duara, 1988) is a defining feature of Chinese ancestor worship. Sangren (2017) explores Chinese deity cults, arguing that these divine beings often originate from real historical figures. They are enveloped in narratives about their life histories and powers, and are revered by followers who testify to their miraculous abilities. Duara (1988) examined the deification of the historical figure Guan Yu (關羽) (or Guangong 關公), whose image evolved across time and space until he ultimately became a popular guardian deity known as Guan Gong. Originally a general during the late Eastern Han Dynasty, Guan Yu was later deified and worshipped across various sectors of Chinese society, including among martial artists, businesspeople, and politicians. His temples are widespread, found not only throughout China but also in Chinese communities worldwide. Duara (1988) argues that while Guan Yu's worship is rooted in history, his characteristics and perceived powers have continually evolved over time, shaped by the needs and values of different periods and groups.

Huangdi is worshipped as a deity across various religious and cultural contexts, particularly within Taoism and folk traditions. His worship is multifaceted, reflecting his legendary status as a cultural hero, sage king, and divine figure. In Taoism, Huangdi is revered as a supreme deity associated with health, longevity, and wisdom, often depicted as a master of alchemy and medicine who attained immortality. Huangdi is closely linked to the development of internal alchemy, and his name is invoked in rituals and ceremonies aimed at spiritual cultivation and well-being. In Chinese folk religion, he is worshipped as a divine ancestor representing the origins of Chinese civilization, honored in rituals for blessings of prosperity, health, and protection. His veneration is particularly evident during cultural festivals, such as the annual ceremonies in Xinzheng, Henan Province, that celebrate him as the mythical progenitor of the Chinese people. Temples dedicated to Huangdi are widespread throughout China and in Chinese communities abroad, serving as sites for offerings, prayers, and rituals that often include recitations of ancient texts attributed to him, such as "The Yellow Emperor's Inner Canon (黃帝內經)," a foundational text in traditional Chinese medicine written between Eastern Zhou and Han

Dynasties. These practices highlight his deep connection to health and well-being. His worship extends to Chinese communities in Hong Kong, Taiwan, Singapore, and beyond, where he is revered alongside other Taoist and folk deities. Temples in these regions often include him in their pantheon of gods, further reflecting his enduring significance in Chinese religious and cultural traditions. The worship of Huangdi as a deity reflects his enduring significance in Chinese culture, both as a legendary figure and as a symbol of divine wisdom and protection.

Today, government-sponsored veneration of Huangdi can be found in several localities, reflecting a revival of public worship from imperial times but presented in a new form. In imperial China, Huangdi was seen as a symbol of legitimate rule and divine authority. By officially worshipping Huangdi, emperors sought to reinforce their own legitimacy, connecting their reign with this revered ancestral figure and solidifying their mandate to rule. The revival of public worship of Huangdi continues to have political significance today, serving as a means to promote cultural unity among the Chinese people, including both mainland and overseas Chinese. By venerating a common ancestor, China aims to foster a sense of shared identity and heritage among its populace.

## The Making of Heritage: Yellow Emperor Ceremonies

While many localities celebrate Yellow Emperor culture today, they all adhere to a standardized process in transforming the Yellow Emperor's legacy into designated heritage. The first is **narrative making**, which is achieved through the reconstruction of historical personas. The Yellow Emperor is treated as a real personality, with efforts focused on reconstructing his life, family lineage, and achievements. These reconstructions draw on diverse historical texts, including canonical and orthodox works, and develop his story as connected to various localities, with each locality contributing its own interpretations. In addition, local governments sponsor archaeological research and initiatives to validate and enhance these narratives. Historical narratives – including textual accounts, oral histories, and findings from recent archaeological research – are often produced and showcased in temples and parks dedicated to the Yellow Emperor, even if they remain unverified in some cases. Academic conferences are organized during the grand ceremonies, inviting local scholars to contribute to the development of locally based narratives. I have participated in these activities in Shaanxi and Henan. Furthermore, these narratives are incorporated into the introductory scripts used by site guides to present the sites and are displayed at heritage sites. For example, the life stories of the Yellow Emperor are featured in every temple, and the different versions of contemporary

"Hundred Family Surnames" maps (百家姓), which identify the Yellow Emperor as a common ancestral figure in the family tree, are prominently displayed. Similarly, souvenirs sold at these heritage sites play a significant role in reinforcing and disseminating this heritage narrative.

The second procedure is **ceremonial making**. While Shaanxi has long had a mausoleum dedicated to the Yellow Emperor, which was designated as a heritage site in 1961 and has hosted ritual worship of Huangdi dating back to imperial times, all the localities discussed in this Element are now creating contemporary grand ceremonies with a set of rituals to honor the Yellow Emperor. The celebration dates are strategically arranged to differ from one another, highlighting the unique contributions of each locality. For example, the ceremony at the Yellow Emperor's Mausoleum in Huangling, Shaanxi, includes twelve steps that were developed in 2003 when the provincial government established an expert group, including scholars in the fields of history, archaeology, painting, sculpture, music, and dance, to create contemporary sacrificial rituals. Both the ceremony in Xinzheng, Henan, and that in Jinyun, Zhejiang, include nine steps, but the sequence and contents of the two rituals are not the same. These ceremonies include traditional elements such as reading sacrificial texts and rituals, as well as modern adaptions including ceremonial gun salutes and cannon firings. These ceremonies blend religious devotion with nationalistic and political strategies, reaffirming connections between the divine, the state, and the people. All these ceremonies are in the process of being designated as ICH within China.

The third is **space-making**. Many heritage projects involve the large-scale creation of parks for hosting temples, grand ceremonies, and monuments in city centers, though many of these were made possible through large-scale relocation. Additionally, many new places and sites are either created or named after the Yellow Emperor and his related ancestors, based on stories associated with him. This is particularly evident in Henan, as observed during my fieldwork, with locations such as Huangdi Date Garden and Huangdi Entertaining Restaurant. These spaces serve both commemorative and educational purposes, strengthening collective memory.

The fourth is branding the locality with the Yellow Emperor culture. In China, cultural heritage has become a key element in branding local identities, often serving as a "name card" for regions seeking to distinguish themselves in both domestic and international markets. Incorporating heritage into local branding can enhance a region's image and provide a connection to its cultural roots, increasing its appeal to tourists, investors, and other stakeholders. Many historical and cultural sites, such as temples, ancient towns, and traditional buildings, are promoting themselves as officially designated cultural heritage and becoming cultural symbols of the region. For example, the ancient city of Xi'an, with its rich archaeological heritage, and the Confucius Temple in Qufu are both central to local branding, showcasing China's historical legacy. Integrating ICH into branding helps Chinese cities and regions build strong, culturally rich identities that promote cultural tourism, attract attention and investment, and contribute to the preservation of their heritage.

## 4 Ceremonies for the Yellow Emperor in Shaanxi, Zhejiang, and Henan

Since the twentieth century, Chinese historians and archaeologists have actively sought the origins of Chinese civilization, a quest that remains central to contemporary discourse on nation-building. Throughout history, records of legendary figures have been deeply embedded in public rituals, festivals, and oral traditions among common people. In exploring related topics, anthropologists have focused primarily on contemporary religious practices, with less emphasis on historical research into these figures and deities. Meanwhile, historians have examined extensive historical records to pinpoint the origins, locations, and significant events associated with deities such as the Yellow Emperor. Localities are competing with each other by referencing various historical sources to claim the Yellow Emperor's birthplace, which might be Xinzheng or Xinmi in Henan Province, or possibly Tianshui in Gansu Province. His burial site is thought to be in Huangling (Shaanxi Province), in Lingbao (Henan Province), in Zhuolu (Hebei Province), in Pinggu (平谷) (a Beijing suburb), in Zhengning (Gansu Province), or in Linfen (Shanxi Province). Consequently, these locations are actively hosting official ceremonies, constructing or reconstructing temples and mausoleums, and transforming them into tourist destinations. They are also applying for recognition of these ceremonies and folk customs as ICH. In addition, contemporary Yellow Emperor temples are found in locations such as Zhijing Mountain (紫荆山), Yangping (陽平) Town, Lingbao City, Henan; Juci Mountain (具茨山) (now known as Shizu Mountain 始祖山), Xinzheng County, Henan; Xinzheng, Zhengzhou, Henan; Xinmi, Zhengzhou, Henan; Hongya Mountain (洪崖山) (formerly known as Houshan Temple 後山廟), Yi County, Hebei; Beishen Mountain (北神山), Shanxi; Zhangzhuang Village (張庄村), Gaoping City, Shanxi; Feixia Mountain (飛霞山), Guangdong; Tianzhu Peak (天柱峰), Jinyun County, Zhejiang; Dongxiang, Tongguan (潼關) County, Yangping, Shaanxi; Hongwei Mountain (洪危), Quyang 曲陽, Shanxi; Huangling County, Shaanxi; Kulong Mountain (窟窿山), Zhuolu

County, Hebei; Xichuan (西川), Qingyang (慶陽), Gansu; Tianshui, Gansu; Yuzi Mountain (漁子山), Pinggu County, Beijing; and Mount Huang (黃山), Anhui, among others (Figure 3). Many temples have started reconstructing their facilities, organizing official ceremonies, and applying for ICH status.

My observations reveal that these locations are leveraging "Yellow Emperor culture (黃帝文化)" as a local brand to bolster their political, cultural, and economic standing. From the perspective of Chinese local governments, this effort aims to enhance tourism and develop regional assets in contemporary China. However, beyond the officials' efforts to boost tourism and political ideology, my fieldwork reveals a genuine local quest to worship China's common ancestors and the deep-rooted oral histories of miracles associated with these locations. Many villages and place names have long been associated with Yellow Emperor (or related) stories, which have been passed down through oral tradition for thousands of years. These memories are a vital part of local transmission and daily life.

Today, three ceremonies honoring Huangdi have been officially recognized as national ICH. The ceremonies in Shaanxi were first designated as provincial intangible heritage in 2005 and upgraded to national heritage in 2006. The ceremonies in Henan were initially listed as provincial intangible heritage in 2007 and elevated to national heritage in 2008. The ceremonies in Jinyun, Zhejiang Province, were named provincial intangible heritage in 2008 and recognized as national heritage in 2011. Since 2012, Mount Huang has been hosting the public ceremony by the provincial government for worshipping the Yellow Emperor, making it the fourth site in China to hold such a grand official ceremony. Several regions also lay claim to Huangdi culture. In the dominant official narrative, the Henan government asserts that Huangdi was born there, while Shaanxi contends that he was buried in its province. Each region uses different historical sources and significant life events to justify its exclusive connection to Huangdi culture. Meanwhile, the Zhejiang government claims that Huangdi was deified there, with temples dedicated to his worship. Among these regions, Henan and Shaanxi host the largest ceremonies, creating a competitive dynamic between their respective governments. Recently, they have been contesting which of their ceremonies should be upgraded to national status (Fang, 2015). Politicians, scholars (including historians and archaeologists), and other advocates from both regions have written academic articles and contributed to news forums to present what they consider to be objective evidence supporting their claims (S.-L.Wang, 2021). In this context, heritage status serves to validate the historical narratives promoted by these localities.

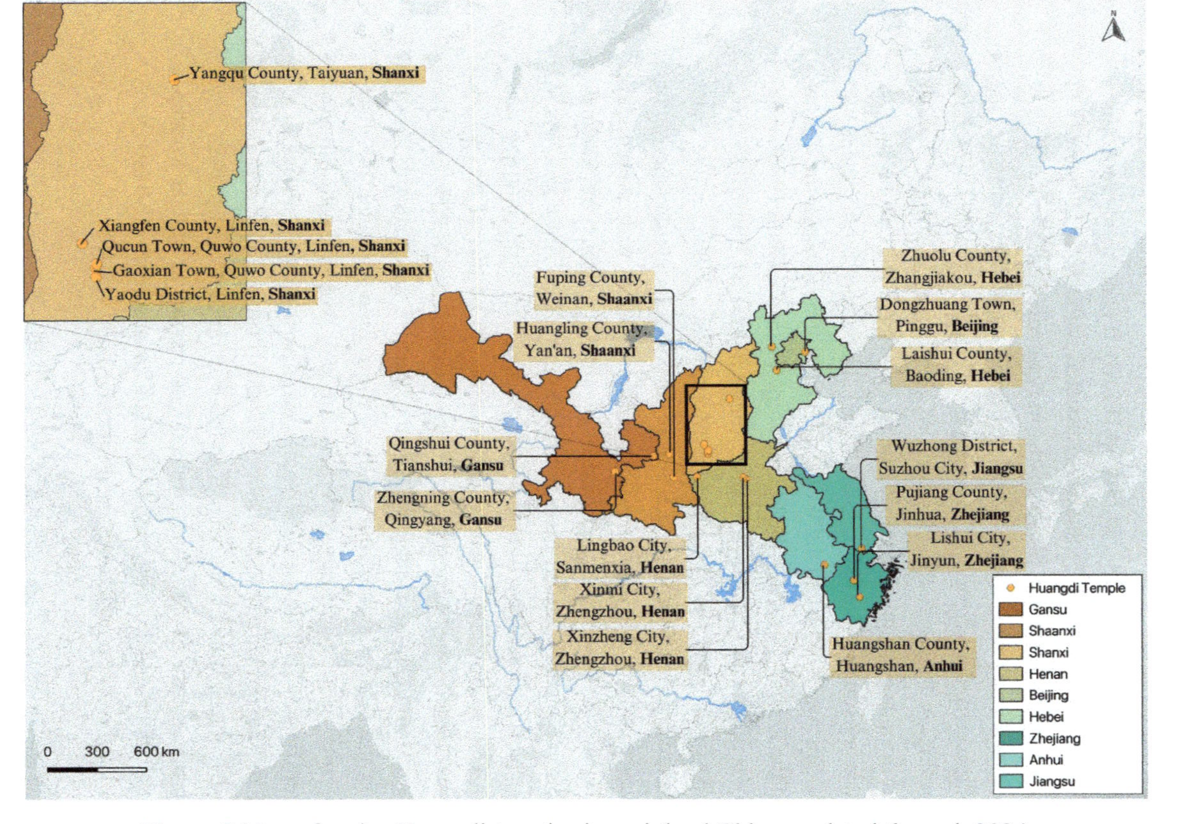


**Figure 3** Map of major Huangdi temples in mainland China, updated through 2024.

**Source:** Compiled by the author.

## The Grand Ceremony for the Yellow Emperor at Huangling in Shaanxi

Huangling County, situated in the southern part of Yan'an, Shaanxi Province, is named after the Yellow Emperor's Mausoleum within the county. It is believed that the mausoleum dedicated to the Yellow Emperor was first established in Huangling during the Han Dynasty (202 BC–AD 220). It underwent renovations in the Tang Dynasty (AD 618–907) and was relocated in the Song Dynasty (AD 960–1279). According to legend, the mausoleum reputedly contains the Yellow Emperor's garments and cap, which were left behind on Mount Qiao after his ascension to heaven and attainment of immortality. The earliest record of Yellow Emperor worship is found in the "Records of the Grand Historian," which mentions that during the reign of King Weilie of Zhou (422 BC), Duke Ling of Qin held a ceremony at this site (Sima Qian, 1996). The record further states that Duke Ling of Qin later established the Wuyang Upper Shrine to honor the Yellow Emperor and the Lower Shrine for the Flame Emperor (Sima Qian, 1996).

The "Records of the Grand Historian: Basic Annals of the Five Emperors" notes that "Huangdi passed away and was buried at Mount Qiao." However, the exact location of Mount Qiao remains debated. Scholars have various interpretations: For instance, sinologist Qian Mu identifies Mount Qiao (橋山) with present-day Shaanxi (Ch'ien, 1978), a view supported by local scholars in Shaanxi. Additionally, some identify Mount Qiao with Zhuolu in Hebei Province, where a temple dedicated to the Yellow Emperor was erected, and with Qingyang and Zhengning in Gansu Province, where a tomb claimed to be that of the Yellow Emperor exists. Despite the existence of various locations for Yellow Emperor worship today, Mount Qiao in Huangling County, Shaanxi, has gradually gained recognition as the official mausoleum of the Yellow Emperor since the Tang Dynasty. The site has a long history of Yellow Emperor worship, with Emperor Wu of the Han Dynasty (202 BC~AD 220) recorded as performing sacrifices there. In AD 770, the Tang Dynasty established national rites to honor the Yellow Emperor at this mausoleum, a tradition that has continued to the present day (Liao, 2016). Subsequent dynasties have maintained records of official worship, sacrifices, renovations, and the protection of Huangdi's mausoleum at Mount Qiao. This national-level worship has been upheld for over 2,000 years.

### *Reviving the Official Worship of the Yellow Emperor in Contemporary Times*

Due to the long-standing tradition of commemorating the Yellow Emperor, many political leaders in the modern period have participated in rituals at Shaanxi's Yellow Emperor Mausoleum. After the Republic of China was established in 1912, Sun Yat-sen, the first provisional president, sent representatives to Shaanxi to honor the Yellow Emperor (Wang, 2006). During the War of Resistance Against Japan (1937–1945), both Nationalist and Communist Party members visited the mausoleum, with Mao Zedong even composing a eulogy in 1937. Following the establishment of the People's Republic of China, the Shaanxi provincial government organized several ceremonies to worship the Yellow Emperor between 1955 and 1962 (Wang, 2006). However, during the Cultural Revolution and subsequent political turmoil, ancestor worship, including veneration of the Yellow Emperor, was banned. It wasn't until the 1980s, when the Chinese government began relaxing regulations on religious activities, that these practices were revived. In 1988, the local Huangling government started holding worship ceremonies at the Yellow Emperor's Mausoleum during the Double Ninth Festival on September 9th. The mausoleum was renovated until 1992, and since 1994, national politicians have annually presided over official worship ceremonies for the Yellow Emperor in Shaanxi. Recently, in 2015, Xi Jinping visited Shaanxi and publicly declared the Yellow Emperor's Mausoleum to be a spiritual symbol of Chinese civilization, emphasizing its significance in tracing Chinese history (Gong et al., 2015). Additionally, in 2009, Taiwanese President Ma Ying-jeou officiated a remote worship ceremony for the Yellow Emperor in Taiwan, emphasizing the importance of respecting ancestors and acknowledging historical origins (Central News Agency, 2024).

Since 2004, the Grand Ceremony has been elevated to an event organized by the Shaanxi provincial government, with participation from central government representatives. The ceremony is now held annually on April 5th, during the Qingming Festival. In 2006, the Yellow Emperor worship ceremony in Shaanxi was designated as national-level ICH, marking its official recognition by the central government. Following the designation of Qingming Festival or Tomb Sweeping Day as national ICH in 2006 and a national holiday in 2008, the mausoleum has attracted many tourists, with the government reporting over 500,000 annual visitors and worshippers at the Yellow Emperor's Mausoleum. In January 2008, the Shaanxi provincial government established the Shaanxi Provincial Work Committee for the Public Sacrifice at the Yellow Emperor's Mausoleum. The committee was created to bolster the organization of public sacrificial activities for the Yellow Emperor, thoroughly explore cultural resources linked to him, and expand and elevate the branding of the Huangdi ceremony. Since 2015, the Yellow Emperor worship ceremony has been held twice a year, on the Qingming Festival and the Double Ninth Festival. Both of these festivals are significant traditional Chinese cultural events where people honor their ancestors by burning incense and offering flowers at gravesites.

To standardize the sacrificial activities at the Yellow Emperor's Mausoleum, Shaanxi Province in 2003 established a "Yellow Emperor's Mausoleum Ritual Research Expert Group," consisting of renowned scholars in history, archaeology, painting, sculpture, music, and dance. The reform plan for the sacrificial rituals proposed by this expert group was reviewed and approved by relevant departments and then implemented. Starting at 9:50 a.m., the ceremony lasts approximately 35 minutes. The new sacrificial procedure specifies the following twelve ritual steps: (1) All participants stand solemnly; (2) Fire ceremonial cannons (thirty-four shots, representing the thirty-four provinces, municipalities, autonomous regions, and special administrative regions of China); (3) Play music; (4) The main officiant assumes their position; (5) The accompanying officiants assume their positions; (6) The main officiant presents incense; (7) Offer wine in a ceremonial cup (the main officiant performs the ritual of offering wine); (8) Present a floral tribute; (9) Read the sacrificial text (read by a professional announcer); (10) Perform three bows; (11) Conduct music and dance performances to conclude the ceremony; (12) Declare the completion of the ritual.

In 2017, I had the opportunity to participate in the Grand Ceremony of the Yellow Emperor in Shaanxi (S.-L. Wang, 2021). The event saw thousands of participants, including politicians, overseas representatives, academic representatives, and student representatives, all of whom were allowed to enter the plaza only with special permits. The ceremonies organized by local governments differ significantly from imperial worship practices. While incense burning and offerings remain central elements of these rituals, the ceremonies themselves are meticulously planned by the local authorities. Performers' costumes are integrated with modern elements, and balloons are suspended in the sky, soaring alongside a dragon that flies into the heavens. Professor Dong from Taiwan, a key figure in designing Taiwan's Confucius worship ceremonies, noted that such ceremonies are conducted according to ancient regulations and have been confirmed by Confucius' descendant Kong Decheng. He observed that grand ceremonies in China are often more entertaining, modern, and joyful compared to those in Taiwan, suggesting that these performances are designed to boost local tourism (personal communication, April 5, 2017).

The media widely reports on the event, not only highlighting its large scale but also emphasizing the emotional significance of people's search for roots and common ancestors in China. In a March 24, 2004 article from the *People's Daily*, Guo Guangchang, head of a private high-tech company serving as the ritual host for private worship for the first time that year, expressed his enthusiasm: "I have always wanted to participate in this event because the cohesion of the Chinese nation has always been the driving force for me and our company. Through the process of worshipping our ancestors, we continually find national self-confidence!" (Mon & Wang, 2004). In the same year, he donated RMB 5 million to renovate the Huangdi mausoleum. The ceremonies dedicated to the Yellow Emperor include eulogies that highlight the importance of ancestor worship and Chinese identity. Recently, these speeches have incorporated political slogans and references to current events. For example, the 2017 ceremony featured the phrase "rolling up sleeves to work hard," directly echoing a public statement by Xi Jinping. Through CCTV broadcasts and newspapers, these ceremonies, featuring traditional customs, national flags, and eulogies that reference various political slogans aligned with each year's political agenda, emphasize the unity of the Chinese nation and strongly reinforce national identity.

In addition to the grand ceremonies, a variety of cultural activities related to the Yellow Emperor are organized. Shaanxi Province hosts events such as concerts themed around Yellow Emperor culture, performances of national songs, and exhibitions. Prior to these major worship ceremonies, conferences promoting Yellow Emperor culture are held in both Henan and Shaanxi. As a cultural heritage research scholar, I attended a conference held in Xi'an, the capital of Shaanxi Province, a few days before the Grand Ceremony in 2017. The conference was themed "Cultural Confidence," reflecting Xi Jinping's 2016 statement advocating for confidence in the path of socialism with Chinese characteristics. Jointly organized by the Institute of Chinese Thought and Culture at Northwest University and the Shaanxi Huangdi Culture Research Association, it was the eleventh conference since its inception in 2007. Scholars from fields such as Chinese philosophy, history, and culture, including several Taiwanese scholars, engaged in discussions on Yellow Emperor philosophy and Chinese culture. Following the conference, all participants took part in the ceremony to honor the Yellow Emperor. Notably, many large conferences in China adopt political slogans as their themes. It is therefore not surprising that slogans like "Finding the roots of Shaanxi and worshipping our ancestor in Huangling" and "Practicing ancestor worship in Huangling as an expression of cultural confidence" were featured prominently at the Shaanxi conference. The Henan conference, held the same year, focused on "Belt and Road, Civilization Interaction," underscoring the continuity of Chinese culture and emphasizing that Chinese civilization is the only one among the four major ancient civilizations that still exists, thus highlighting the importance of tracing its roots.

At the same time, exhibitions and calligraphy displays were held at cultural palaces and museums, including special exhibitions such as the one on the Shimao and Yangguanxhao sites at the Shaanxi History Museum in Xi'an in 2016. The exhibition, titled "Searching for Huangdi Culture: Shimao and Yangguanzhai Sites (黃帝文化尋蹤-楊官寨、石卯考古發現的啟示)," implied a connection between Huangdi and the sites through its name and explicitly made this link in the exhibition content (Shen, 2017). It provided context for the Yangguanzhai and Shimao sites, which date back to the Yangshao culture (仰韶文化), approximately 5000 to 6000 BP, when the Huangdi Clan is believed to have had activities in the area. Moreover, during the conference commemorating the Yellow Emperor in 2017, local historian Mr. Hu attempted to connect the Shimao site with Yellow Emperor culture, suggesting that it was established by the Yellow Emperor's clan (Hu, 2017). Despite skepticism from the archaeologist community, this view was supported by local historians such as Mr. Hu, who advocated linking Shimao with Huangdi, and Mr. Huo, who supported connecting archaeological discoveries in Baoji, Shaanxi, with Yandi. Both were subsequently invited to the 2017 Yellow Emperor Culture Conference. Some archaeologists leading the excavation have made connections between the site and Huangdi, while other archaeologists have dismissed these speculations as mere conjecture (personal communication, April 10, 2018).

## Making Place with Huangdi Culture in Huangling

The Yellow Emperor's Mausoleum area covers 333 hectares and contains over 60,000 ancient cypress trees, with more than 30,000 being more than 1,000 years old, making it the most well-preserved cypress grove in China. The site is divided into two main sections: the mausoleum and Xuanyuan Temple (軒轅廟). The mausoleum area features the Hong Kong and Macau Handover Monuments and various inscriptions by historical and modern figures. Xuanyuan Temple, which includes the temple and the main sacrificial hall, was rebuilt after 1993. The area also includes sites linked to Huangdi's legend, such as the renovated Huangdi temple used for ceremonies, the "Huangdi Planted Tree (黃帝手植柏)," which is said to have been planted by the Yellow Emperor, and a large footprint attributed to him. Initially, Shaanxi's claim to Huangdi culture was based on the Yellow Emperor Mausoleum, where it was believed that his garments had been buried since the Tang Dynasty, and where various dynasties held official ceremonies. Today, the narrative at the mausoleum tourist site has expanded: the government asserts not only that the Yellow Emperor was physically buried in Huangling but also that he left a footprint and planted a tree there 5,000 years ago.

Additionally, local archaeological narratives are evolving and influencing Shaanxi's historical claims. Over time, Shaanxi's association with Yellow Emperor culture has been reinforced by support from devotees and discoveries such as the Yangguanzhai and Shimao sites. The narrative has shifted from viewing Huangling merely as the burial site of the Yellow Emperor to recognizing it as a significant location associated with his activities. While tourist sites often present Huangdi as a historical figure based on stories from historical sources, local archaeological narratives tend to depict Huangdi as a clan associated with local sites. The current status of the Yellow Emperor worship ceremonies in Shaanxi as national ICH reflects this consolidation of Shaanxi's claims. The local government now emphasizes Huangling as a key site of the Yellow Emperor, further solidifying its exclusive rights to Huangdi culture through ongoing official ceremonies and evolving archaeological narratives.

## The Grand Ceremony for the Yellow Emperor at Jinyun in Zhejiang

During the Tang Dynasty under Empress Wu Zetian (武則天), in AD 696, a new county named "Jinyun" was established in Jinyun, Zhejiang, named after the Yellow Emperor's title "Jinyun Clan." Jinyun is the only county on the mainland named after the Yellow Emperor. According to a local guide, the Yellow Emperor had three palaces: Mount Huang, Mount Lu, and Jinyun Mountain (personal communication, July 2023). Jinyun is believed to be the place where the Yellow Emperor ascended to heaven. When further asked, the guide said: "Legend has it that Shaanxi Huangling emphasizes the place where the Yellow Emperor was buried after his death and where his physical body ascended to heaven, while Jinyun is the place where the Yellow Emperor, as a deity, ascended to heaven after becoming an immortal" (personal communication, July 2023). Dinghu Peak (鼎湖峰), associated with the Yellow Emperor's casting of tripods and refining of cinnabar, is said to be the location of his ascension. Since the Yellow Emperor is also known as the supreme ruler, there are fifty-nine steps leading up to Dinghu Peak.

The site is known for its beautiful scenery and is nestled among mountains. It has long been a sacred place in Daoism. The history of worshipping the Yellow Emperor here dates back to AD 423 when the Eastern Jin literatus Xie Lingyun wrote in his "Records of Famous Mountains (名山記)" about the "Jinyun Hall (縉云堂) in Yongjia," over 1,600 years ago. During the Tang Dynasty under Emperor Xuanzong, Jinyun Mountain was officially renamed Xiandu Mountain (仙都山), and Jinyun Hall was designated as the Yellow Emperor's temple. In the Northern Song Dynasty (AD 960–1127), it was renamed Yuxu Palace (玉虚宮). Over the centuries, the site has seen numerous inscriptions and records from over 400 poets, totaling more than 1,000 poems. It has experienced various periods of damage and reconstruction. By the Qing Dynasty (AD 1644–1911), the Yellow Emperor's temple was deteriorating (Xiao et al., 2022). Additionally, archaeological findings have supported the ritual activities in the area. In 1997, archaeologists discovered copper dragon wood tablets in Jinlong Cave (金龍洞), and in 2022 a Northern Song Dynasty golden dragon measuring 3.3 cm was found (Xie & Wang, 2023).

Many local villages also have dragon-related names. According to the Xiandu Gazetteer (仙都志) of the Yuan Dynasty (AD 1271–1386), Daoist and sacrificial activities were documented in the area as early as AD 1020 during the Northern Song Dynasty.

Already in 1994, the Jinyun County government applied to develop the site into the Xiandu Scenic Area and to reconstruct the Huangdi Temple (黃帝祠宇). This plan was approved by the Ministry of Construction, and publicworship resumed in 1998, establishing the "Northern Tomb, Southern Temple" pattern. In 2011, the ceremony worshipping the Yellow Emperor was designatedas a third batch national ICH. In 2014, it was officially preserved as a festival project by the Zhejiang Provincial Party Committee and the State Council.

Since the construction of the scenic area in 1998, two annual ceremonies have been held – the Qingming Festival for public worship and the Double Ninth Festival for official worship – contrasting with the timing of events organized in Shaanxi. Initially organized by the Jinyun local government, the official ceremony came under the purview of the Zhejiang provincial government in 2021, officially becoming a regular event. In 2023, the ceremony's theme was "Promote Yellow Emperor Culture, Unite National Spirit." It was led by the vice governor of Zhejiang Province, with the former vice chairman of the Kuomintang Party from Taiwan and over a hundred Taiwanese participants in attendance.

For 2024, the public ceremony held on the Qingming Festival featured a cross-strait joint worship of the Yellow Emperor, themed "Same Roots, Same Ancestors, Cross-Strait Joint Worship" (Lin, 2024). The Double Ninth Festival ceremony in 2024 focused on dragon culture, with Dinghu Peak being the legendary site where the Yellow Emperor ascended on a dragon. The ceremony typically begins at 9:50 a.m. and includes nine rituals: (1) long-horn blowing (with nine horn players blowing five times each); (2) drum and bell striking (thirty-four drumbeats and fifteen bell rings representing China's thirty-four provinces and autonomous regions and the 1.5 billion descendants of the Yellow Emperor worldwide); (3) offering high incense; (4) presenting flower baskets; (5) offering fine wine; (6) reciting the sacrificial text; (7) performing a bowing ceremony; (8) singing hymns; and (9) performing music and dance rituals. Guests at the ceremony are given yellow ribbons to wear. In addition to the ceremony, an academic conference on Yellow Emperor culture and literate Du Guangting studies was co-hosted with the Fudan University Center for Ancient Literature Studies and the Department of Chinese at East China Normal University.

Contemporary Zhejiang Province is actively promoting Jinyun's Huangdi culture and developing tourism around elements related to the ancestral figure of Huangdi. For example, in 2022, the 15th Party Congress of Zhejiang Province emphasized the need to "create new cultural and artistic symbols and enhance the influence of traditional cultures such as Yangming Culture, Harmony Culture, Yellow Emperor Culture, Dayu Culture, Southern Confucian Culture, Wu-Yue Culture, and Zhejiang Studies." Among these, the Yellow Emperor, Dayu, and Confucius are considered remote ancestral figures. Moreover, the region has established the Chinese Overseas International Cultural Exchange Base and the Cross-Strait Exchange Base. According to my visit to the tourist center in the scenic area in 2023, there are many photos of important Taiwanese figures and businessmen who have visited the site for ancestor worship and tours. The local government has also developed the local Wu opera (婺劇) performances with themes such as "Xuanyuan Feitian (軒轅飛天)," "Xuanyuan Praise (軒轅贊)," and "Xuanyuan Ode (軒轅頌)" in the scenic area. Additionally, Yellow Emperor-themed health food, a Yellow Emperor Culture Garden, and a provincial-level Yellow Emperor Culture Academic Committee are being prepared. Local residents have opened a cultural creative shop named "Bringing Celestial Spirits Home," selling various Yellow Emperor-themed products, including sacrificial items, stationery, cakes, and surname culture merchandise.

The scenic area was reconstructed in 1998, with most villages either preserved within the area or rebuilt elsewhere. Many of these villages have been converted into guesthouses or hotels. In the coming years, the villages within the scenic area will be merged into one – Jufeng Village (巨峰村). During my conversations with villagers in the area, I learned that many do not have a strong impression of the Yellow Emperor Temple, viewing it as a reconstruction. Some acknowledge that it may have existed in the past but was destroyed long ago. Most local villagers rarely engage in worship there, showing greater devotion to the Guanyin Temple instead. Despite the limited local worship of the Yellow Emperor Temple, "Huangdi culture" is just one component among many, and the tourism industry has significantly developed the area. According to Xiao et al. (2022), in 2021 the village collective income of Dinghu Village (鼎湖村), a core area within the scenic area, reached 1.32 million yuan, with an average disposable income per resident exceeding 30,000 yuan.

Since 2024, there has been a call from Jinyun for a three-site joint worship, with Shaanxi Huangling, Henan Xinzheng, and Zhejiang Jinyun beginning to collaborate on this three-site worship initiative. However, it has not yet been realized.

## The Grand Ceremony for the Yellow Emperor at Xinzheng in Henan

Xinzheng, a county-level city located in the north of Henan Province, is now under the administration of the provincial capital, Zhengzhou. Xinzheng is considered to be one of the birthplaces of the Chinese nation. The city got its name during the Zhou Dynasty for being the capital of the states of Zheng and Han (鄭韓). Xinzheng and Henan Province are rich in archaeological culture. About 8,000 years ago, during the Neolithic period, the Peiligang (裴李崗文化) culture left its mark in the region. According to local legend, 5,000 years ago, the legendary ancestor Huangdi was born in Xinzheng and established the Youxiong (有熊) Kingdom. In the "Records of the Grand Historian: Basic Annals of the Five Emperors" compiled in the Han Dynasty, it is recorded: "The Yellow Emperor, son of Shaodian (少典), had the surname Gongsun and the given name Xuanyuan. The Yellow Emperor resided at the Hill of Xuanyuan." In the "Records of Emperors and Kings" by Huangfu Mi (皇甫密) of the Western Jin Dynasty, it is stated: "The Yellow Emperor, of the Youxiong clan, was the son of Shaodian and belonged to the Ji surname. [He was born in] Youxiong, which is now Xinzheng in Henan." Some scholars have debated and identified Xuanyuan Hill and the Youxiong Kingdom as today's Xinzheng. Recently, extensive archaeological studies have been conducted to examine this legend.

In the late 1980s, ancestral worship, along with related temples and religious practices, experienced a widespread revival across China, flourishing significantly (Chau, 2006). Since the 1990s, the Xinzheng local government has hosted an annual cultural celebration in the city center, combining festivities with tourist promotion dedicated to the Yellow Emperor. In 2006, the Henan provincial government began to lead official worship ceremonies for the Yellow Emperor in Xinzheng. That same year, the event was listed as provincial-level ICH. In 2008, it was elevated to national ICH by the State Council. This ceremony, one of the largest in the country, encourages a billion Chinese people to worship their ancestors. This event takes place at an old temple dedicated to the Yellow Emperor, which has been renovated and is now surrounded by a newly constructed park that features a new statue of the Yellow Emperor. The celebration typically includes a variety of cultural activities, ceremonies, and performances aimed at honoring the Yellow Emperor and promoting the rich historical and cultural heritage associated with him. The renovated temple and the new statue serve as focal points for these festivities, symbolizing the enduring legacy of the Yellow Emperor in Chinese culture.

In the city center, a new park has been established, featuring a giant statue of Huangdi encircling an old temple dedicated to him. At Juci Mountain, where legends say Huangdi was born and numerous oral histories have been passed down in the surrounding villages, a temple has been rebuilt to honor and worship Huangdi. The government organized a ceremony dedicated to Huangdi on his birthday, which is March 3rd, according to the Chinese calendar. Meanwhile, local people pay homage to Huangdi at Juci Mountain during the Double Ninth Festival, which includes a week-long temple fair.

In April 2017 and 2018, I was invited to attend the grand worship ceremonies held on the third day of the third lunar month, the birthday of the Yellow Emperor. The theme of the ceremony in 2017 was "Same Root, Same Ancestor, Same Origin; Peace, Harmony, and Concord." More than 10,000 Chinese from over 40 countries participated in the event in Henan that year. Additionally, during this period, a series of activities took place, including exhibitions of Chinese calligraphy and paintings, as well as the Yellow Emperor Culture International Forum.

Although organized by the Henan provincial government, the event's significance was underscored by the invitations sent to overseas Chinese, symbolizing the announcement that the Yellow Emperor is the common ancestor of Chinese people worldwide. This Grand Ceremony was hosted by the Henan provincial government in collaboration with various organizations, including the Overseas Chinese Affairs Office of the State Council, the Henan Provincial Committee of the Chinese People's Political Consultative Conference, the Yan Huang Culture Research Association, the All-China Federation of Returned Overseas Chinese, the All-China Federation of Taiwan Compatriots, the Zhengzhou Municipal People's Government, and the Xinzheng Municipal People's Government.

Waking up at 6 a.m. in both 2017 and 2018, attendees, including me, had to undergo strict security checks, with handbags not allowed. We waited several hours until 9:50 a.m., when the ceremony began with the ringing of bells in numerical patterns referencing the honorable Chinese emperors. The annual Grand Ceremony includes nine major worship rites: (1) firing guns in salute; (2) wreath-offering; (3) lighting incense sticks; (4) paying homage to the ancestors; (5) reading eulogies; (6) singing odes; (7) dance performance; (8) blessing of the homeland; and (9) celebrating harmony among heaven, Earth, and human beings. However, despite being listed as national intangible heritage, the Grand Ceremony for Huangdi is a contemporary creation organized by the government. Worship rites such as the saluting of guns, reading eulogies, singing odes, and dance performances are modern innovations. In this new form of remote ancestor worship, traditional religious practices have been transformed into a series of modern national symbolic rites for public display. Across China, remote ancestral cults are similarly organized by various levels of local governments, each adopting different formats to replace traditional practices. For instance, the Huangdi ceremony in Shaanxi features twelve rites, while the one in Zhejiang features nine rites.

Two features of the ceremonies drew my attention. First, the oral narratives assert that Huangdi is the common ancestor of all Chinese people, including various ethnic groups, suggesting that we, as his descendants, have a duty to preserve and promote Huangdi's culture. Second, souvenirs sold in shops around the park for the Huangdi ceremony prominently feature the "hundreds of surnames." These items, such as fans and key rings, display local surnames, with shop owners explaining that all Chinese surnames trace back to Huangdi, reinforcing the notion that everyone is a descendant of Huangdi.

In contrast to the official annual ceremony of Huangdi, which adheres to fixed rites established by local officials, local people practice worship in a more traditional manner. On the Double Ninth Festival, people gather at a small temple of the Yellow Emperor on Juci Mountain in the suburb of Xinzheng, where there is no set ceremony. This Huangdi temple was largely rebuilt and renovated in the 1990s, with new statues installed.[4] During this period, people from neighboring villages began visiting the temple regularly on the first and the fifteenth of the lunar month, bringing food and flowers on the Double Ninth. Local worship practices are simpler and more traditional – they involve burning incense, offering food, and placing flowers. Many locals hope that their ancestor Huangdi will bring them good fortune. Villagers often visit the temple to honor Huangdi and express their wishes. Additionally, tourists from various parts of China come to see Huangdi, whom they know from news and travel brochures to be a common ancestor of the Chinese people. These visitors pay their respects with a simple gesture of palms together and take photos with the colossal statue of Huangdi.

After participating in the Grand Ceremony in Xinzheng in 2017 and 2018, I revisited the site several times outside these events. It increasingly felt like a tourist attraction, lacking grassroots participation. This impression shifted somewhat after the COVID-19 pandemic.

When I visited again in August 2023, the Yellow Emperor park had been closed to the public for three years and access was restricted to high officials with a government introduction letter. During this period, construction continued, with two new museums and a renovated plaza being completed in the park. I was surprised to learn that the surrounding neighborhood continued to visit regularly to worship the Yellow Emperor from outside the gate. I was even more astonished to see a woman kneeling outside the closed site, burning

---

[4] During my fieldwork, local archaeologists explained that part of the foundation of the temple unearthed at Juci dates back to the Spring and Autumn period (771–476 BC), and some bricks are from the Han Dynasty (202 BC–AD 220). Although repeated destruction and rebuilding over time makes it difficult to determine the temple's original construction date or the identity of the main deity, the display board next to the temple states that the temple was built in the Spring and Autumn period.

incense through the wire fence toward the direction of the Yellow Emperor Temple. Inside, I encountered a group of about twenty middle-aged women from Zhengzhou who had privately arranged entry with a cleaner. They had laid out a national flag with five stars, placed offerings on it, and read their own ceremonial texts. Although they did not know each other personally, they were part of a WeChat group that organized such religious activities, charging 150 yuan per trip. Midway through their ceremony, a site leader arrived, expelled them for conducting superstitious activities, and then welcomed another government group with a special introduction letter for a visit and worship.

## Popular Memories of Huangdi and Promoters of Huangdi Culture

The revival of Huangdi worship in Henan has been a grassroots initiative driven by local efforts, contrasting sharply with the top-down approach in Shaanxi. In Shaanxi, the official Huangdi ceremony has been established since the Tang Dynasty, with local governments historically responsible for maintaining the mausoleum and hosting ceremonies. To promote Henan's claim to Huangdi culture, two individuals have been crucial: Zhao Guoding and Liu Wenxue (personal communication, 2017, 2018). Zhao, known locally as Zhao Huangdi, dedicated his life to establishing Xinzheng as Huangdi's hometown. I interviewed Zhao in 2017 when he was eighty-three years old.

Zhao's journey began in 1983 during a business trip to Hainan Island. There, he met Mr. Huang from Henan Village, who claimed that his lineage originated from Xinzheng and that their ancestor was Huangdi. Moved by this, Zhao remembered the dilapidated Huangdi Temple in his hometown and felt that it was a disgrace for such an important figure's temple to be in ruins. Despite skepticism and the taboo associated with linking Huangdi to mythical and feudal times in the early 1980s,[5] Zhao decided to renovate the temple. Facing resistance and losing his job amid ridicule, Zhao used his own resources to gather historical evidence and petition various levels of government.

His efforts gained momentum with the support of Taiwanese businessman Zhao Haijing, who helped convince the Xinzheng government to renovate the temple in the early 1990s. This support came at a time when Taiwan had just abandoned martial law, and many Chinese-born Taiwanese citizens were returning to China to worship their ancestors. The renovation was partly driven by the political significance of strengthening ties with Taiwan and overseas Chinese. By the early 1990s, Xinzheng began organizing the first Huangdi cultural

---

[5] The term for emperors in Chinese is written as 皇帝 and pronounce as huangdi, while the term for Yellow Emperor is written as 黃帝 and also pronounce as huangdi.

tourism festival, with Zhao overseeing the event as part of the city's cultural bureau. Zhao renovated the temple in the city center of Xinzheng, which had been converted into a veterinary hospital during the Cultural Revolution, and also restored the old temple at Juci Mountain, where stories about Huangdi's birth were celebrated. At the 2017 provincial Huangdi ceremony, Zhao was honored as a bearer of China's ICH for his contributions and continued to participate in the ceremony annually until his death in 2018.

The second key figure in promoting Huangdi culture is Mr. Liu Wenxue, who wrote the popular 1990s novel *China's First Great Emperor*, featuring Huangdi as the central character. I collected various narratives, stories, and origin myths of Huangdi from local villagers in Juci Mountain, near Xinzheng. Interestingly, many locals linked their stories of Huangdi to Liu's novel and the popular film *The Yellow Emperor*. Shop owners around tourist sites like the Park of the Yellow Emperor (黃帝故里) and the Huangdi Temple (軒轅故里祠) inside the park often shared stories similar to those in official brochures and museums. In rural China, legends and myths about Huangdi are presented through oral histories, dramas, and popular religion.

Several individuals have devoted their efforts to revitalizing Huangdi culture, driven by a patriotic passion for advancing Chinese heritage. In addition to the two figures identified by the local cultural bureau, Mr. Ky Liao, an Indonesian-born American Chinese with a deep commitment to Chinese heritage, has been a significant force in promoting Huangdi culture in Henan. By 2015, Liao had donated over RMB 600 million to four Chinese universities and established a research center for Huangdi culture. Collaborating with Mr. Xu, head of the Association for the Study of Yandi and Huangdi Culture in Beijing, Liao has lobbied to elevate Henan's Huangdi ceremony to a national-level event. In 2016, during China's "Two Sessions (兩會)," Liao proposed that the national Huangdi ceremony be held in Beijing, with a local ceremony in Xinzheng, and advocated for adopting the Huangdi chronology in place of the Gregorian calendar (Xu, 2015). He has also funded the construction of a park promoting a healthy lifestyle based on the Huangdi Sijing medical texts (黃帝四經), a collection of Daoist writings from the Western Zhou period discovered at the Mawangdui (馬王堆) archaeological site in 1973 in Changsha, Hunan. Through his assistance, I learned that Liao views Huangdi culture as a scientific philosophy and incorporates concepts from physics, such as Einstein's theories, to interpret both the universe and Huangdi's philosophy (personal communication, 2017). He believes that promoting Huangdi's philosophy, rather than Confucian culture, will improve how Chinese culture is perceived; thus, he advocates for exercise based on the Huangdi Sijing.

In promoting Huangdi as a national ancestor and branding Henan as his hometown, all the individuals involved share a strong commitment to celebrating Chinese cultural roots and honoring Huangdi to enhance national pride. This effort reflects a common trend in China, where people from the same hometown often develop a deep local identity. For instance, Taiwanese businessmen and Beijing officials who assisted Mr. Zhao, as well as Mr. Xu, have all contributed to elevating Henan's status through Huangdi culture. Today, thousands of people, both migrants and expatriates, return to their hometowns annually to participate in ancestor worship and related events.

### *Making Place with Huangdi Culture in Xinzheng*

Henan's Xinzheng has long promoted itself as the birthplace of Yellow Emperor culture. Xinzheng city is served by an international airport, which is the principal airport for Zhengzhou, capital of Henan Province. Upon arriving in Xinzheng, visitors are greeted by signs on both sides of the road, proclaiming "Welcome back to Huangdi's hometown" and "Worshipping the Chinese ancestor Huangdi." Henan Province now defines itself as the common ancestral root and spiritual homeland of Chinese people, both in the country and abroad. Colossal statues of Huangdi are prominently displayed at several major locations in the city to symbolize his historical significance. The annual Huangdi ceremony has evolved into a major tourist festival for Xinzheng, drawing thousands of visitors each year to celebrate Huangdi's birthday. A government official proudly shared that the ceremony has significantly boosted the city's appeal for investment, thanks to the associated economic and trade activities. As of 2016, it is estimated that a total of USD 153.9 billion has been invested in Xinzheng and Zhengzhou.

The project of the Park of the Ancient Home of the Yellow Emperor was started in 1997, and 5,000 square meters of land were relocated and greened. In 2002 and 2003, the site was expanded to 430,000 square meters, and in 2007 it was further expanded to accommodate the needs of the Huangdi Hometown Ancestor Worship Ceremony. To make way for the newly built Park of the Yellow Emperor in the center of Xinzheng, where the ancient Huangdi Temple once stood, the city's most prosperous historic district was dismantled, and hundreds of thousands of people were relocated. The park now features a vast, gleaming cement plaza dominated by a new statue of Huangdi. The new areas include the Chinese Surname Plaza, the Xuanyuan Hometown Temple Forecourt Area, the Xuanyuan Hometown Temple Area, the Ancestor Worship Area, the Xuanyuan Hill, and the Yellow Emperor Memorial Hall Area.

The Temple of the Yellow Emperor is situated in the center of the park. The temple area covers approximately 2 mu (about 1,333 square meters) and features a main hall with five rooms. In the main hall sits a statue of the Yellow Emperor, with a plaque inscribed "The First Ancestor of Humanity (人文始祖)." The back wall and the east and west walls are adorned with murals depicting the life of the Yellow Emperor. The temple also has three auxiliary halls on both the east and west sides. The east hall features a statue of Leizu (嫘祖), the primary wife of the Yellow Emperor, while the west hall has a statue of Mozu (嫫祖), the secondary wife. Nearby stands a monument by the World Hakka People's Association for Ancestor Worship. The front courtyard has three rooms that display archaeological cultures, ranging from Peiligang culture, through Yangshao culture, to the Longshan (龍山) culture of Xinzheng. These displays implicitly reflect the corresponding archaeological periods matching the life activities of the Yellow Emperor. The earliest archaeological remnants date the temple foundation to the Han Dynasty, but it was not until the Ming Dynasty that it was clearly used and constructed. The Temple of the Yellow Emperor was listed as a Henan Provincial Important Heritage Site in 2003.

The Chinese Surname Plaza in the southernmost part of the park was newly constructed in 2007. This area features a bronze Yellow Emperor's Treasure Cauldron Altar and a Chinese Surname Wall. The Chinese Surname Wall is inscribed with the top 100 surnames published in 2006 and over 3,000 surnames with historical records. In this park, visitors can find various commemorative items related to surnames, illustrating the different Chinese surnames, with the central origin tracing back to the Yellow Emperor.

The Ancestor Worship Plaza is located behind the temple and serves as the main venue for the Huangdi Hometown Ancestor Worship Ceremony. The central feature is a 36-meter-wide path of deep red granite with a "Five Colored Earth (五色土)" pattern that leads up to the statue of the Yellow Emperor. On either side of the plaza are long corridors adorned with about 200 couplets. To the north of the plaza are the Chinese Sacred Flame Platform, the Ancestor Worship Platform, and the Song Platform.

The Yellow Emperor Memorial Hall is located under the legendary Xuanyuan Hill and consists of two floors, with a total building area of 30,018 square meters. The first floor is underground, where the central feature is a 5.9-meter-tall bronze statue of the Yellow Emperor, symbolizing the highest respect with the "nine-five" significance.

Notable sites in Xinzheng include the Huangdi Internal Medicine Memorial Hall (黃帝內經博物館) with the association with the Yellow Emperor's Inner Canon and Huangdi's Ancient Date Garden (黃帝棗園), known for its red dates and said to be where Huangdi led his ministers in planting date trees. Other significant sites include the Fuxi Mountain Grand Canyon, the Yellow Emperor's Immortal Cave (黃帝洞), and Ling Mountain (Heavenly Cave), all promoted as locations where the Yellow Emperor performed sacrificial rites. Additionally, the Huangdi Eternal Love theme park (黃帝千古情) features a large statue of the Yellow Emperor, ancient-style streets, snacks, souvenirs, and amusement facilities. The park also includes a 3,300-seat theater that hosts a large-scale song and dance performance narrating the Yellow Emperor's legends, spanning from the 1942 Henan Famine to contemporary Zhengzhou development.

During the local development process, a series of large-scale demolitions, reconstruction of scenic areas, and the assignment of new place names can be observed. This process imparts symbolic significance to the areas, transforming them to align with the new cultural and historical narratives being established. The development efforts deeply link the area with Huangdi culture and legend, creating a narrative that integrates historical significance and cultural symbolism into the local landscape. This helps to reinforce and celebrate the area's association with Huangdi, embedding the legend into the physical and cultural fabric of the region.

## Rivalry in Branding Huangdi Culture within Henan Province: The Case of Huangdi Palace in Xinmi

Within Henan Province, the competition to establish and promote Huangdi culture has created a notable rivalry, particularly among Xinzheng, the adjacent Xinmi (bordered by Juci Mountain), and Lingbao. While Xinzheng has successfully positioned itself as the birthplace of Huangdi, Xinmi has also sought to capitalize on its historical and cultural connections to the Yellow Emperor.

In neighboring Xinmi, efforts to associate with Huangdi culture are evident. The Huangdi Palace (黃帝宮), formerly known as Yunyan Palace (雲岩宮) from the Ming Dynasty, has been rebranded to emphasize its connection to Huangdi. Historically, the Tang Dynasty official Du Guji (獨孤寂) erected the "Feng Hou's Eight Formation Diagrams Monument (風后八陣圖記)" to highlight the strategic importance of the Eight Diagrams developed by Huangdi and Feng Hou (風后). Ming Dynasty poet Zhang Yuji (张于阶) also praised the site in his poem "Pacing through Feng Hou's Formation (贊黃帝宮八陣詩)."

Xinmi has leveraged historical and literary claims to market the area as "The First Palace under Heaven (天下第一宮)," positioning it as a significant site related to Huangdi (Liu, 2006). The local government has promoted the site by linking it to the "Eight Trigrams (八陣圖)" of Huangdi, citing sources like the "Records of the Grand Historian" and the "Classic of Mountains and Seas (山海經)" to suggest that it was where Huangdi built palaces, trained troops after battles with Chiyou, and created the Eight Trigrams. Some claims even suggest that it is where Huangdi met his wife, Leizu. The site is also promoted as the birthplace of Huangdi and the location where he established his palace. Declared a provincial scenic area in 2007, the Yellow Emperor Palace, along with the Derby Ski Resort, has been managed by a private tourism company since the pandemic to promote holiday tourism. Despite its historical claims, many of the ancient-style buildings of the Yellow Emperor Palace in Xinmi are new constructions. The newly constructed palace features several courtyards, including a training ground and various ceremonial buildings, and emphasizes its branding. Key structures include the Commanding Terrace, the Palaces, the Xuanyuan Gate, the Lecture Hall Gate, as well as the Ancestor's Cave (人祖洞), the Nine-Dragon Pond (九龍潭), and Leizu Hall (嫘祖草堂). The Ancestor's Hall (祖師殿), once a site for worshipping deities such as the Three Pure Ones (三清) and the Ancestor, was destroyed during the Cultural Revolution. Today, the Ancestor's Cave, which features statues of Huangdi and his minister Feng Hou, is marketed with historical texts that claim Huangdi's presence there.

Xinmi's branding is reinforced by these archaeological discoveries and local legends. During construction in 2008, an ancient cultural site was discovered with pottery shards including net-patterned black pottery, eggshell pottery, and tripod legs, which are believed to be from the early Longshan culture, around 4,700 years ago. Additionally, the third national cultural relics census uncovered a large ancient site north of the Yellow Emperor Palace, the Ancient City Site (古城寨遺址), spanning artifacts from the Peiligang, Yangshao, and Longshan cultures. The Ancient City Site, excavated by the Henan Provincial Archaeological Team, revealed large-scale palace buildings from the Longshan culture. This site has been promoted as the capital of the Yellow Emperor, Xuanyuan Hill (軒轅丘), by the local government. The Ancient City Site was recognized as one of the Top Ten Archaeological Discoveries of 2000 and was listed as a key cultural heritage protection unit in the fifth batch of national cultural relics in 2001. However, due to financial constraints, further protection and development of the site have been limited.

During my visit in August 2023, I initially had doubts about the authenticity of the area's historical significance due to the newly constructed buildings at the Yellow Emperor Palace. However, I later discovered that many local place names are linked to the Yellow Emperor. These names – such as Ma Ji Ling ([馬驥嶺], the Yellow Emperor's horse training ground), Cang Wang Zhuang ([倉王庄], the alleged residence of Cang Jie [倉頡], Huangdi's historian according to legend), Yangmazhuang Village (養馬庄), Moqishan ([摩旗山], where Huangdi planted a flag), Qibaishan (岐佰山), and Caochanggang ([草場崗], a storage place for Huangdi's grains) – reinforce the area's deep connection to Yellow Emperor legends and cultural heritage. Nearby, the old Tianxian Temple (天仙廟) is now in ruins, and the area awaits further tourism planning. The Juci Mountain area surrounding Xinzheng, Xinmi, and Yuzhou (禹州) is part of this ongoing development.

The rivalry with Xinzheng persists, with both cities vying to enhance their association with Huangdi to attract tourism and investment. However, as the official noted, Xinzheng has successfully branded itself as Huangdi's birthplace, has been listed as a national ICH site, and hosts ceremonies to reinforce this identity. The Henan provincial government prefers to avoid internal rivalries and conflicts within the province, which might complicate efforts to present a unified cultural heritage narrative. As a result, the official narrative positions Xinzheng as Huangdi's birthplace and Xinmi as the place where Huangdi began his career.

## Rivalry in Branding Huangdi Culture within Henan Province: The Case of Huangdi Mausoleum in Lingbao City

The Huangdi Mausoleum in Lingbao, also known as the Jing Mountain Huangdi Mausoleum (荊山黃帝陵) or the Huangdi Casting Cauldron Plain (黃帝鑄鼎塬), is located 20 kilometers west of Lingbao City on Jing Mountain. In 2000, it was listed as part of the third batch of provincial-level cultural heritage protection units. As of August 2023, although the site has been developed, the surrounding scenic area and its additional attractions are still under planning. The "Records of the Grand Historian, Volume 28: Fengshan Book (封禪書)" describes how Huangdi, using copper from Shou Mountain, cast a cauldron at the foot of Jing Mountain (荊山). Upon completion, a dragon descended to greet Huangdi. Huangdi mounted the dragon, and the dragon ascended with him, leaving the smaller officials behind. These officials held onto the dragon's beard, which was pulled off and fell onto Huangdi's bow. The people believed that Huangdi had ascended to heaven with the dragon and thus named the place Dinghu and the bow "Wuhao." The casting of the cauldron at Jing Mountain and the ascent of Huangdi are also recorded in historical texts such as "Book of Han: Rituals" (漢書·郊祀志) and "Commentary on the Water Classic." While there are five mountains named Jing in China today, scholars have referenced "The Book of Chow (尚書)," which states: "Jing and He both refer to Yuzhou [in Henan]; Jing is Lingbao's Jing Mountain."

Legend has it that people buried the Yellow Emperor's boots on Huangdi's Casting Cauldron Plain, forming the Yellow Emperor's Mausoleum. Later, they established the Tomb of the Yellow Emperor's Clothing (衣冠塚) at this site and built a temple for worship. For thousands of years, many scholars and officials have left their footprints and documentation here.

The site of the Huangdi Temple is believed to be where Emperor Wu of the Han Dynasty constructed the Dinghu Palace (鼎湖宮), and there is a Huangdi Casting Cauldron Plain behind it. There is also a Tang Dynasty stele inscribed by Wang Yan (王顏), the governor of Guozhou (虢州), and written by Yuan Zhiliu (袁滋籀), the governor of Huazhou (華州) and Inspector-General, titled "Inscription on the Casting Cauldron Plain of Xuanyuan Huangdi (軒轅黃帝鑄鼎原碑銘並序)." The stele, discovered in 1978 during a cultural heritage survey in Daziying Village (大字營村 or 達紫營村) of Lingbao County, was found in three broken pieces, with only the main body remaining. It was moved to the Huangdi Casting Cauldron Plain in 1995. This Tang Dynasty inscription is the earliest known record of Huangdi's deeds, dating back more than 700 years earlier than similar inscriptions found in Huangling County, Shaanxi Province. According to the guide in 2023, local legend has it that during the construction of the mausoleum, a jade pendant was unearthed at a depth of 4 feet. This pendant was sent to the Tang Dynasty court, where officials debated its origin, concluding that it was from the time of Huangdi rather than the Han or Qin dynasties. Consequently, those who found the jade were awarded official positions. In addition, many literati throughout history have written about it. For example, the famous poet Li Bai (李白), in his work "Feilong Yin Ershou (飛龍引二首)," wrote: "The Yellow Emperor cast a tripod on Jing Mountain and refined cinnabar. The cinnabar turned into gold; riding a dragon, he flew to the Great Pure Home, leaving behind clouds of sorrow and seas of thoughts (黃帝鑄鼎於荊山, 煉丹砂。丹砂成黃金, 騎龍飛去太清家, 雲愁海思令人嗟)." Chen Zi'ang's (陳子昂) poem "Xuanyuan Tai (軒轅台)" includes the line "Climbing the Ji Hill in the north to look out, seeking the ancient Xuanyuan Platform (北登薊丘望, 求古軒轅台)."

According to the local chronicle "Wenxiang County Gazetteer (閿鄉縣誌)," "The Yellow Emperor's Tomb is located on the casting tripod site in the south of the county." In 1992, the local government established a mausoleum for the Yellow Emperor and later made three tripods in front of the renovated temple: the Heaven Tripod, the Man Tripod, and the Earth Tripod.

The billboard at the site particularly emphasizes that the area around the Yellow Emperor's Tomb is rich with over thirty sites of the Yangshao culture. For example, the nearby Beiyangping site (北陽平遺址) is a Neolithic settlement, identified as part of the fifth batch of cultural heritage units in 2001. Part of the Beiyangping site is the Xipo site, covering an area of 4.36 square kilometers, with copper ore from the Yangshao period, approximately 5,500 years ago. In 2004, the Xipo site (西坡遺址) was listed as one of the top 100 major archaeological sites for protection during the Eleventh Five-Year Plan. It was also recognized as one of the top ten archaeological discoveries in China in 2006 and as one of the six major sites in the Source of Chinese Civilization

Project (Jiang, 2023; Li, 2010). According to a book published by the Henan Provincial Archaeological Team, the Xipo site might be associated with the Huangdi period (Chen, 2012). In April 2024, Lingbao City hosted a conference on the excavation results of the Beiyangping site and an academic seminar on Yellow Emperor culture. The event featured a lecture by Li Xinwei (李新偉) from the Institute of Ancient History at the Chinese Academy of Social Sciences, titled "The Yangshao Culture from a 'Multifaceted Unity' Perspective (多元一體是腳下的仰韶文化)," and a presentation by Cao Bingwu (曹兵武), vice president of the China Yanhuang Culture Research Association.

In additional to archaeological culture, many nearby village names are also related to the Yellow Emperor, such as Loudi Village (婁底村), Palou Village (爬婁村), Qiaoying Village (喬營村, named after the mother of the Yellow Emperor), Miaodi Village (廟底村), Sangyuan Village (桑園村), and Chousang Village (稠桑村), indicating the teaching of mulberry cultivation for silkworm rearing by the Yellow Emperor's wife Leizu. Xujiaying Village (徐家營), where the Yellow Emperor's horse and other items were placed after his ascension, also shows this connection, and the surname Ma is prevalent in this village (personal communication, August 2023). Additionally, Gantou Village (幹頭村), Dongce Village (東冊村), Xice Village (西冊村), Dachang Village (大常村), and Xiaochang Village (小常村), as well as the name of the township, Yangping Town (陽平鎮), indicate the center where the Yellow Emperor measured the spring and autumn equinoxes (Jiang, 2023).

Lingbao's Yellow Emperor legend was recognized as provincial ICH in 2006. Although Henan Province is rich in archaeological culture and local oral histories, the province does not want internal competition over the Huangdi culture brand. The tour guide introduced: "The Yellow Emperor was born in Xinzheng, rose to prominence on Jing Mountain, and was buried in Shaanxi." On April 22, 2023, the "Guimao Year Lingbao Yellow Emperor Casting Tripod Ancestor Worship Ceremony (癸卯年灵宝黄帝铸鼎原拜祖大典)" was held, under the theme "Same Roots, Same Ancestors, Same Source; Peace, Harmony, and Concord (同根同祖同源, 和平和睦和谐)." It took place on the same day as the ceremony in Xinzheng, with branches in Lingbao, Jiyuan, Xinmi, and other locations in Henan. Participants also sang the "Huangdi Song (黃帝頌)" together (He, 2023). The same day featured a Yellow Emperor culture seminar and a week-long Yellow Emperor Temple Fair. Later, on January 29, 2024, Xu Haixing (許海星), a member of the Henan provincial political government and chairman of the Sanmenxia (三門峽) Municipal Committee, formally proposed at Henan Province's political gathering Two Sessions, to establish a sub-venue for the Grand Ceremony of Huangdi at the Huangdi Casting Cauldron Plain in

Lingbao City, Henan Province, during the annual March 3rd Yellow Emperor Ancestral Worship Ceremony held in Xinzheng, the Yellow Emperor's hometown (Yang & Kan, 2024).

In summary, the competition between Xinzheng, Xinmi, and Lingbao within Henan Province over their connections to Huangdi culture exemplifies the broader trend of regional rivalry in promoting cultural heritage in China. Each city leverages historical claims, archaeological evidence, and modern development to assert its association with Huangdi, reflecting a wider effort to capitalize on cultural heritage for reasons of economic benefit and regional pride.

## 5 Making Heritage and Transforming Historical Narratives

### The Pursuit of Common Ancestors

How can the rise of these popular new ancestral cults be explained? In our time, the pursuit of a common origin and the imagining of an ancestor for all Chinese people, including those overseas, is driven by the aim of eliminating differences among them, thereby creating a sense of homogeneity and identity. Alongside China's reform and economic and political growth, the country takes pride in its rich culture and long tradition, aspiring to expand its influence internationally. The state's policy has fueled a national fervor and a search for roots, fostering an imagined political "we" based on kinship relations, as all Chinese are considered to be descendants of Yandi and Huangdi. China claims a 5,000-year history as a civilization, reviving the discourse of autochthonous ancestors to support this claim. In this new narrative, which is part of the public discourse, all Chinese are said to be descended from the Yellow Emperor, despite the lack of a clear genealogy. Official heritage discourse is employed to legitimize the status of the Yellow Emperor and various other remote ancestors, igniting the cult of remote ancestors among ordinary people and local communities. This has resulted in the creation of legitimate statues of Huangdi and other legendary ancestors, along with various government-sponsored grand ceremonies and celebrations.

The contemporary cult of Huangdi is not an isolated phenomenon but is linked to the broader national essence fervor and the rise of Chinese nationalism. This movement is rooted in a new era of ideological transformation, China's increasing global prominence, and the drive to unify Greater China. After attending various ceremonies and events honoring Huangdi in Shaanxi, Henan, and other regions, I observed that the inclusion of overseas Chinese participants has become a key element. This practice symbolizes the unity of people worldwide in honoring their common ancestors. Each year, national leaders and representatives from Hong Kong, Macau, Taiwan, and overseas

Chinese communities are invited to these ceremonies, emphasizing their role in asserting a shared origin and fostering a collective cultural heritage. Particularly noteworthy is how the cult of Huangdi is received in regions with ethnic minorities, where conflicting views of Chinese nationalism have surfaced. For example, the Miao ethnic group in Southwest China has revered the "uncivilized" Chiyou, identifying themselves as his descendants defeated by Han Chinese, as a means of reconciling with the Huangdi origin myth. In Northwest Gansu Province, near Xinjiang, local government initiatives have also promoted the Huangdi cult. However, it remains unclear how people with different historical perspectives engage with and respond to the Huangdi myth. The rise of Chinese nationalism and the push to create a "homogeneous" Chinese ethnicity – transforming a Han-centric history into a pan-Chinese identity – may be perceived as a threat by ethnic minorities who hold alternative historical narratives.

Thompson (2014, p. 60) asserts that "an eponymous ancestor – in contrast to a heroic ancestor – derives his name directly from that of a people" and notes that "once created, the eponymous ancestor has a life of his or her own, independent of the group or place which lay at its origin. Subsequent tales about this ancestor may either totally lack such a historiographic meaning, or this element in the narrative might be reduced to a mere 'point of attraction.'" An eponym refers to a person, place, or thing after which something is named. This can be seen in ancient Greece and the Bible, where notable figures or heroes were used to name places or periods. For example, Ishmael was the progenitor of the Ishmaelites, and Argos was named after the king of Argos. In this context, Huangdi, or the Yellow Emperor, serves as an "eponymous" figure, regarded as the progenitor of the Yellow Chinese race and influencing the name of the Huangdi period and its associated culture. In Xinzheng city, traditionally considered Huangdi's hometown, the Huangdi period replaced the Yangshao culture by endowing Xinzheng with an eponymous identity through its connection to Huangdi.

I argue that cultural heritage not only serves as a source of national pride, underscoring China's greatness, but also plays a crucial role in legitimizing long-standing Chinese historical narratives. David Lowenthal (2018, pp. 121, 132) asserts that heritage and history use fundamentally different methods of persuasion. History often involves exaggeration, omission, invention, and forgetting – relying on ignorance and error – while heritage involves crafting a revised version of historical legacies that is essential for shaping identity. Heritage adapts history to contemporary contexts, highlighting and celebrating positive aspects while downplaying or omitting elements considered shameful or harmful (Lowenthal, 2018, pp. 148–172).

## The Role of Archaeology in Promoting Huangdi Culture

Today in China, the wealth of historical materials and ongoing archaeological discoveries have significantly extended the known history of the nation. Influenced by the School of Doubting Antiquity, which calls for a more skeptical and critical examination of historical sources and ancient China, the introduction of archaeology in the early twentieth century enabled Chinese scholars to apply scientific methods to uncover material evidence of Chinese history. Field research and archaeological findings are now considered a "new texture of evidence," playing an auxiliary role in supporting Chinese historiography (see Bagley, 1999; Chang, 1981; Von Falkenhausen, 1993). As Fiskesjö (2006) points out, while traditional historiography claims that China has a 5,000-year-old history, only 3,000 years have been archaeologically verified. Scholars from the School of Doubting Antiquity, such as Gu (Wagner, 2019), have questioned the historical validity of the period extending from 5,000 to 3,000 years ago, suggesting that it may be mythical. In contrast, Li Xueqin (李學勤) (2008) notes that archaeology is part of the "School of Interpreting Antiquity (釋古學派)," which focuses on interpreting and understanding ancient Chinese historical texts and traditions using material evidence. This approach helps extend the origins of Chinese civilization by addressing periods that scholars from the Doubting Antiquity School have dismissed as mythical. Archaeological fieldwork on this prehistory in the Yellow River Valley is an attempt by Chinese scholars to validate the 5,000 years of history that are claimed. The ancient period of China has particularly captivated Chinese archaeologists as it helps pinpoint the origins of Chinese civilization. While tracing the origins of agriculture or human development, archaeologists may point to various times and locations within China. However, when it comes to the origins of dynastic China, which are rooted in the Three Sovereigns and Five Emperors, it is still widely believed that they are centered in the Yellow River region. The renowned archaeologist Xia nai (夏鼐) noted that Chinese archaeology is a branch of history and argued that it must sever connections with earlier historical studies. Mao's principle of "making the past serve the present" continues to influence Chinese archaeology.

Since the reform, the establishment of provincial archaeological museums, cultural heritage institutions, and regional archaeological teams has fostered a more localized approach. Von Falkenhausen (1995, p. 202) observed that this new regionalist paradigm in Chinese archaeology emerged from bureaucratic restructuring. This regionalized administration can enhance regional archaeological narratives by emphasizing local elements and connecting them with ancient ethnonyms and national identities. With numerous historical texts available, historians have frequently attempted to identify and connect contemporary places with those mentioned in ancient records. Since the 1980s, rising nationalism and the restructuring of state power have led to increased regionalism, resulting in localities competing for the rights to historical place names. This competition often involves using heritage discourse to justify their "ownership" of historical figures, such as remote ancestors, and to construct a sense of place. For example, Jinba (2013) discusses the discovery of an ancient "queendom" recorded in classical Chinese texts, highlighting how these regional claims are made.

Efforts to connect archaeological findings with ancient ethnonyms and local identities are evident in this research. The figure of Huangdi is especially prominent in Henan and Shaanxi, where local scholars strive to link regional archaeological sites to places associated with Huangdi. While historical sources date Huangdi to around 2700–2600 BC, some scholars have linked the legendary era of Huangdi described in historical records with the Neolithic archaeological period of Yangshao culture, due to their overlapping time frames. In Shaanxi, for example, scholars have associated the Shimao and Yangguanzhai archaeological sites with Huangdi's clan (compare with Hu, 2017). Additionally, exhibitions on Shimao culture were held concurrently with the official Huangdi ceremonies to suggest a connection between the site and Huangdi. In Xinmi and Lingbao of Henan, both areas emphasize their local Xipo and Guchengzhai sites as potentially linked to the footsteps of Huangdi. In Xinzheng, archaeologists discovered rock paintings on Juci Mountain, a site associated with the legend of Huangdi's birthplace and the location of the Huangdi Temple. Although some archaeologists have noted privately that the dating suggests these rock paintings were created in a later period, the local government continues to attempt to link Juci's rock paintings to Huangdi. Ironically, despite Huangdi being credited as the founder of agriculture, the earliest site with agricultural evidence, dating back to 8000 BC, is the Hemudu site in southern China. The current understanding of the Yellow Emperor is based primarily on legends and ancient texts written in much later periods, rather than on concrete archaeological evidence (Wagner, 2019). While today's archaeological research, largely supported by local governments, attempts through interpretation to link the various legends of Huangdi with actual archaeological findings, this process remains fraught with uncertainty and challenges.

Despite not having ample support, local museums have presented their findings in connection with distant mythical ancestors. At the Xinzheng Museum of Henan, the exhibition frequently associates various Neolithic cultures in Henan with mythical figures, as observed during the author's visit in

2019. An introductory text highlights the archaeological sites related to both Yangshao and Huangdi cultures. Additionally, the Peiligang culture is linked to the Shaodian period, the Yangshao culture is associated with the Huangdi period, and the Longshan culture references figures such as Zuanxu, Diku, Yao, and Shun. A map even tracks the purported footprints of Huangdi, associating all Yangshao sites found in Xinzheng with Huangdi's legends and renaming them accordingly. According to the head of the Xinzheng Museum, it is challenging to definitively link any site in the region to Huangdi culture, and responsible archaeologists should be cautious about making such claims. However, as the museum is part of the local government, it is obligated to provide these interpretations (personal communication, 2018).

How could Huangdi, as an individual, be responsible for leaving so many footprints not only across Henan Province – in Xinzheng, Xinmi, and Lingbao – but also in Shaanxi, Zhejiang, and other regions with historical claims of his presence? Today, some archaeologists propose that Huangdi might not be a personal name but rather a surname for an entire clan. This theory could explain why historical texts state that Huangdi lived for 300 years, why he is attributed with numerous significant Chinese cultural inventions, and why he is said to have visited so many locations across China. A local official in Xinzheng remarked, "Archaeologists and historians are increasingly convinced that Huangdi was born in Henan because the region is traditionally regarded as the cradle of Chinese culture, with the Yellow River running through it" (personal communication, 2018). Similarly, the worship of the mythical ancestor Yao has been practiced in Shanxi, where the local Taosi (陶寺) archaeological site in Linfen is interpreted as being the capital from the Yao period (He, 2021). Recent scholarship has highlighted the nationalistic tendencies in Chinese archaeology (compare with Trigger, 1995). However, further research is needed to explore how sponsorships, "provincialism," and the "regional paradigm" (Levenson, 1967; Von Falkenhausen, 1995) are influencing archaeological practices and interpretations in China, contributing to the current competition among localities.

Today, numerous archaeological excavations and findings indicate that Chinese civilization emerged from multiple origins (Fei, 1989; Su & Yin, 1981). In this context, archaeology plays a crucial role in identifying the origins of early China, particularly when sites are presented as evidence of Huangdi's existence. Local governments have leveraged their own archaeological sites and cultural artifacts to support the claim that Huangdi culture existed in their regions. While the terminology used by archaeologists for these sites remains unchanged, local officials and historians are working to establish these connections. Although the past is represented through various forms and narratives, archaeology remains the most compelling method for the Chinese government to substantiate the nation's historical claims. Historians, archaeologists, and museum curators all have the potential to influence and reshape contemporary historical discourse.

In a global context where collective identity is increasingly expressed through culture – such as distinctive lifestyles, traditions, and forms of art or craft – public museums and officially designated sites of heritage serve as powerful representations of local culture and history, as observed in the Chinese case. Today, as new historical narratives emerge at heritage sites and museums, we see a shift in how Chinese history is portrayed. While many Chinese archaeologists and contemporary textbooks maintain a conservative stance, there is a growing trend of linking Chinese history to national mythologies.

## The Rivalry of *Histories*

Thanks to the UNESCO heritage discourse that brands places with heritage honors, we are now seeing rivalries in China over the ownership of cultural heritage related to ancestors, celebrities, and historical figures. Localities aim to brand themselves by associating with these figures through applications for ICH status, organizing public ceremonies in their honor, creating large-scale cultural parks, and claiming exclusive rights to their cultural significance. Empowered by heritage discourse, localities are competing to claim exclusive rights to the cultural heritage associated with their regions. They are doing this through various heritage designations, including customs, festivals, and oral histories related to these figures. In the case of Huangdi, rivalries are evident among provinces such as Shaanxi, Henan, Zhejiang, Gansu, and Shandong. Additionally, within Henan Province, there are rivalries among places like Xinzheng, Lingbao, and Xinmi, each claiming their own rights to the legacy of Huangdi. Localities competing for the title of Huangdi culture each build their case based on "objective" historical facts. As demonstrated, various agents develop different versions of these historical narratives, leading to multiple competing histories. In this context, there are multiple rival versions of *histories*. In Shaanxi, Henan, and Zhejiang provinces, each employs distinct historical canons to justify its regional histories and establish unique identities. Within a locality, archaeologists and historians often have differing perspectives on the past, leading to varying types of knowledge and standards of validation. In Xinzheng, Henan, for instance, the narratives presented in museums and by tourist guides frequently diverge from the archaeological interpretations. There is no single method for constructing a culture; local historians' interpretations are sometimes supported by local governments to promote regional history.

Although historical narratives traditionally rely on local canons and oral histories, popular memory of Huangdi in Xinzheng has been influenced by a novel written in the 1980s. Thus, both the novel and popular memory contribute to the creation of historical narratives. Local-based narratives are crafted from historical sources, while archaeology and tangible materials are used to support these arguments. Archaeologists and historians often find themselves in disputes over the truth, with local myths evolving from various historical writings and oral histories. People's historical memory is shaped by oral traditions passed down through generations, intertwining with contemporary historical and archaeological knowledge.

In popular discourse, Huangdi is often portrayed as a real historical figure with a well-defined genealogy and documented activities, rather than just a mythological figure or deity. Tourist sites, monuments, statues, shows, and movies frequently highlight Huangdi's identity as a historical individual. Conversely, in archaeological discourse, Huangdi is more commonly accepted as a clan from prehistory, associated with the Yangshao culture and lasting for approximately 300 years.

The role of Huangdi has evolved significantly over time. Originally revered as the first ancestor of the imperial family in imperial China, Huangdi was later recognized, in the early twentieth century, as the ancestor of the Han Chinese people. Today, observations from contemporary Huangdi ceremonies suggest that the government aims to promote Huangdi as the ancestral figure for all Chinese people, including ethnic minorities. This narrative supports the idea of a unified origin for Chinese civilization, whether linked to Shaanxi Province or to Henan Province. Additionally, contemporary heritage discourse has embraced the Yellow Emperor ceremony, granting it official recognition and reinforcing associated narratives. Consequently, there is a noticeable disparity between academic and popular discourses regarding the origins of Chinese civilization.

Officially, this discourse is employed to promote the notion of a unified Chinese state. This nationalist-driven approach to cultural heritage construction seeks to present China as a nation with continuous history, enduring traditions, and a rich cultural legacy. A notable aspect of this process is how localities are developing their own cultural heritage to forge distinctive regional identities and brands.

## New Religious Practices

Notably, this Element finds that in the new form of remote ancestral cults, the designation of an ancestor is based not on kinship or blood ties but on regional connections. Such figures are worshipped not as territorial gods with efficacy tied to specific communities (e.g., Feuchtwang, 1992; Lin, 1988) or the locations of their followers and temples, which may not align with administrative boundaries; rather, these remote ancestors are venerated for their historical connections with contemporary administrative regions – such as towns, cities, or provinces – where they had significant ties during their lifetimes, including their birthplace, their burial place, or their place of business.

Interestingly, some of these newly recognized ancestral figures are not worshipped in traditional temples, although new temples are being built for them. Instead, they are venerated through large statues in public plazas and modern ceremonial rites. Moreover, these religious cults either are already classified as ICH at various governmental levels or are in the process of applying for such status. During my fieldwork in China, I observed localities competing over the "ownership" of these figures and the associated "culture."

The dynamics between central and local authorities in China have been thoroughly examined by anthropologists and sinologists. Historically, when the imperial government officially recognized a particular cult, like the Mazu cult (as noted by Watson, 1985), it not only granted official status to the deity and temple but also increased their perceived power. Such recognition was seen as an extension of imperial authority and a method of local social control (Sangren, 2000, pp. 45–68). Competing temples often create alternate histories to strengthen the spiritual influence of their particular deity or temple. This practice is still evident in modern Mazu cults in Taiwan, where various temples assert their roles as historical authorities and claim connections to the original temple in Meizhou (Sangren, 2000). As Sangren (2000, p. 66) stated, "official recognition, in whatever form, of a local cult effectively legitimizes that cult's corresponding community in the eyes of the state and, to the extent that the state is viewed as legitimate and prestigious, enhances the community's status relative to its neighbors." Rivalry between local temples in Taiwan at pilgrimage cult centers can weaken the circular reasoning that allows the Mazu cult to simultaneously legitimize both state and local institutions. These local centers actively compete for dominance, with officials and leaders vying for influence, while also striving to legitimize themselves through pilgrimage cults to the mother temple in Meizhou, the birthplace of Mazu (Sangren, 2000, pp. 64–68, 76).

Localities in China employ various strategies to assert their authenticity. In the case of the contemporary Huangdi cult, each area develops its own narrative, drawing on diverse historical sources to substantiate its connection to Huangdi. They then hold large-scale ceremonies designed to attract attention, with high-profile guests and media coverage elevating each event's prominence. The ceremonies must obtain official local, provincial, national, or even global UNESCO World Heritage status. Achieving national heritage status, backed by the central government, boosts the locality's prestige, draws investment, and promotes tourism. Additionally, local officials and historians seek to connect their archaeological sites with Huangdi by inviting scholars, particularly state archaeologists, to local conferences to bolster their claims to Huangdi culture.

In contemporary China, records about common ancestors are closely connected to popular religious practices, historical traditions, and oral histories. McNeal (2021) suggests that ethnographic studies focusing on current rituals may overlook important historical context. Conversely, historians examining historical documents to trace the origins and events related to these figures might neglect modern practices. This highlights the need for a more integrated approach that considers both historical and contemporary aspects in the study of religion in China, as demonstrated by the present Element.

## 6 Conclusion: Making Place Through Heritage Branding

In this Element I have presented an ethnography of new religious phenomena in contemporary China, focusing on large-scale remote ancestral cults observed in various localities. Firstly, this Element argues that these remote ancestor cults reflect the broader UNESCO heritage boom in China, where localities are designated as having distinguished cultural value and heritage status. Secondly, this Element highlights a surge in remote ancestor worship across China, spearheaded by local governments. These initiatives involve constructing monuments, temples, sculptures, and parks, as well as staging large-scale ceremonies to honor mytho-historical figures such as Huangdi, Yandi, and Dayu. These activities, endorsed as significant expressions of remote ancestral cults through public ceremonies, underscore the blending of traditional rituals with contemporary practices. A key characteristic of contemporary religious activities in China is their cultural and economic value; they feature a "public display" aspect that appeals not only to adherents but also to a broader audience that is seeking entertainment. In modern China, the popular market for religious tourism is distinguished by its cultural and historical appeal, incorporating entertaining elements rather than purely religious ones. Religious pilgrimage has become part of cultural tourism, where the pursuit of authenticity is less important than the quest for entertainment. These ceremonies are framed as local customs and heritage rather than superstitions by the central state (Ashiwa, 2009, p. 59; Oakes & Sutton, 2010). As illustrated in this Element, the creation of large-scale remote ancestral cults by local governments is driven not by religious beliefs but by the desire to showcase place-based identity and to reinforce local boundaries in China.

The emergence of local cults commemorating ancestors and temples was driven not solely by economic incentives or top-down efforts; instead, as this Element demonstrates, in Henan some activities originated with local individuals who were driven by a patriotic passion to honor their nation and hometowns. For example, Zhao Guoding devoted his time and resources to reviving Huangdi worship, motivated not by personal gain but by a patriotic ideal and a desire to contribute to his hometown and country. His commitment, along with that of many others who have similarly invested in their localities, facilitated the revival of these traditions. These individuals have been dedicated to promoting locally based identities and connecting their regions to a broader national history and identity.

This Element reveals that localities are increasingly using the name card of Huangdi to define themselves, reflecting a broader heritage discourse aimed at branding localities with their claimed heritage. Many of these large-scale ancestral cults are in the process of applying for heritage status, with state recognition of such cults as intangible heritage following the endorsement of the Convention for Intangible Cultural Heritage in 2004. The contemporary cult of Huangdi is part of the revival of "Huangdi culture" that has become a key branding tool for many Chinese localities. In Xinzheng today, nearly everything – from companies and food to souvenirs – is associated with Huangdi culture. This association serves to promote Huangdi culture, helping the region stand out and distinguishing it from others, reflecting the cultural heritage boom in contemporary China.

By commemorating a locality's origins through its famous ancestors, local identities and histories are constructed and branded. The eponymous nature of Huangdi allows the Huangdi culture to be claimed and owned. Echoing Handler (2011), who points out that nations are perceived to hold cultural traits that shape their identity and legitimacy, this ethnography demonstrates how localities in China, similar to individuals, are developing unique identities through their cultural heritage.

In conclusion, this Element argues that the Yellow Emperor cult is driven by nationalism, a widespread grassroots movement for tradition and religious revival, as well as the global trend of heritage discourses that bolster national identity through the creation of heritage. Together, these forces are contributing to the resurgence of ancestral cults, positioning them as vital components in contemporary China's assertion of cultural and historical identity. Legacy encompasses not only the preservation of the past but also the selection and interpretation of historical narratives. This is achieved, as revealed by this Element, through the selective adoption of ancient texts and contemporary archaeological findings that are then showcased in heritage sites and museums to promote "historical knowledge." The narrative surrounding the Yellow Emperor demonstrates that historical knowledge is deeply embedded in the social contexts from which these memories emerge. Both history and heritage serve as representations of the past and play a pivotal role in shaping present identity. This Element has shown how the discourses of myth, history, and heritage-making are intrinsically linked to the discourse of identity, and how UNESCO-driven heritage discourse has taken root, fostering a new form in contemporary China.

# Appendix
# Chinese Chronology

| | | |
|---|---|---|
| Prehistory | Three Sovereigns and Five Emperors | 2900–2100 BC, Uncertain |
| | Xia Dynasty | c. 2070–1600 BC (texts recorded, not yet archaeologically proven) |
| Shang Dynasty | | 1554–1046 BC (texts recorded, archaeological time is from the sixteenth to the eleventh centuries BC) |
| Western Zhou Dynasty | | 1045–771 BC |
| Eastern Zhou Dynasty | Spring and Autumn Period | 770–481 BC |
| | Warring States Period | 480–221 BC |
| Qin Dynasty | | 221–207 BC |
| Western Han Dynasty | | 202 BC–AD 220 |
| Xin Dynasty | | AD 9–24 |
| Eastern Han Dynasty | | AD 25–220 |
| Period of Disunion | | AD 220–589 |
| Sui Dynasty | | AD 589–618 |
| Tang Dynasty | | AD 618–907 |
| Song Dynasty | | AD 960–1279 |
| Yuan Dynasty | | AD 1279–1368 |
| Ming Dynasty | | AD 1368–1644 |
| Qing Dynasty | | AD 1644–1911 |

# References


Anagnost, Ann. (1997). *National Past-Times: Narrative, Representation, and Power in Modern China*. Durham, NC: Duke University Press.

Anderson, Benedict. (1983). *Imagined Communities*. London: Verso Books.

Ashiwa, Yoshiko. (2009). Positioning Religion in Modernity: State and Buddhism in China. In Yoshiko Ashiwa and David L. Tank, eds., *Making Religion, Making the State: The Politics of Religion in Modern China*. Stanford, CA: Stanford University Press, pp. 43–73.

Bagley, Robert. (1999). Shang Archaeology. In Michael Loewe and Edward Shaughnessy, eds., *The Cambridge History of Ancient China*. Cambridge: Cambridge University Press, pp. 124–231.

Berliner, David. (2012). Multiple Nostalgias: The Fabric of Heritage in Luang Prabang (Lao PDR). *Journal of the Royal Anthropological Institute*, 18(4), 769–786.

Callahan, W. A. (2005). Nationalism, Civilization and Transnational Relations: The Discourse of Greater China. *Journal of Contemporary China*, 14(43), 269–289.

Carrico, Kevin. (2017). *The Great Han: Race, Nationalism, and Tradition in China Today*. Oakland: University of California Press.

Central News Agency. (2024). Qingming ji xuanyuan huangdi Ma ying-jeou: biao da tai wan ren dui zhong hua wen hua zhong shi. *Udn.com*, April 4 [online]. Available at: https://udn.com/news/story/8946/7877573 [accessed April 7, 2024] (in Chinese).

Chang, Kwang-chih. (1981). Archaeology and Chinese Historiography. *World Archaeology*, 13(2), 156–169.

Chau, Adam Yuet. (2006). *Miraculous Response: Doing Popular Religion in Contemporary China*. Stanford, CA: Stanford University Press.

Chau, Adam Yuet. (2009). Expanding the Space of Popular Religion: Local Temple Activism and the Politics of Legitimation in Contemporary Rural China. In Yoshiko Ashiwa and David L. Tank, eds., *Making Religion, Making the State: The Politics of Religion in Modern China*. Stanford, CA: Stanford University Press, pp. 211–240.

Chen, Ailan. (2012). *The Cradle of Huaxia Civilization Henan-China*. Henan Provincial Bureau of Cultural Heritage. Zhengzhou: Wenxin.

Chen, Jingguo. (2010). Minsuxue yihuo renleixue? Zhongguodalu minjianxinyang yanjiu de xueshu quxiang [Folklore or Anthropology? Academic Approaches to the Study of Folk Beliefs in Mainland China]. In Minsu yu wenhua bianjibu, ed., *Minsu yu wenhua*. Taipei: Boyangwenhua, pp. 21–47.

Ch'ien, Mu. (1978). Huangdi [The Yellow Emperor]. Taipei: Dongda (in Chinese).

China Intangible Cultural Heritage Network and China Intangible Cultural Heritage Digital Museum. (2024a). Guojiaji feiwuzhi wenhua yichan dai-biaoxing xiangmu daibiaoxing chuanchengren. Available at: www.ihchina.cn/representative#target1 [accessed July 17, 2024] (in Chinese).

China Intangible Cultural Heritage Network and China Intangible Cultural Heritage Digital Museum. (2024b). Guojiaji feiwuzhi wenhua yichan dai-biaoxing xiangmu minglu. Available at: www.ihchina.cn/project.html#target1 [accessed April 7, 2024] (in Chinese).

Cohen, Alvin P. (2012). The Origin of the Yellow Emperor Era Chronology. *Asia Major*, 25(2), 1–3.

Dikötter, Frank. (1992). *The Discourse of Race in Modern China*. Oxford: Oxford University Press.

Duara, Prasenjit. (1988). Superscribing Symbols: The Myth of Guandi, Chinese God of War. *Journal of Asian Studies*, 47(4), 778–795.

Duara, Prasenjit. (1995). *Rescuing History from the Nation: Questioning Narratives of Modern China*. Chicago, IL: Chicago University Press.

Fang, Guanghua. (2015). Where Should the National Ceremony Be Held? *Ta Kung Pao*, September 10 [online]. Available at: http://news.takungpao.com.hk/mainland/focus/2015-09/3159818_print.html [accessed January 1, 2019] (in Chinese).

Faure, David. (2007). *Emperor and Ancestor: State and Lineage in South China*. Stanford, CA: Stanford University Press.

Fei, Xiaotong. (1989). *The Plurality and Organic Unity of the Zhongghua Minzu*. Beijing: Zhonggua Renmin Xueyuan Chubanshe (in Chinese).

Feuchtwang, Stephan. (1992). *Popular Religion in China: The Imperial Metaphor*. Abingdon: Routledge.

Fiskesjö, M. (2006). Rescuing the Empire: Chinese Nation-Building in the Twentieth Century. *European Journal of East Asian Studies*, 5(1), 15–44.

Gadamer, Hans Georg. (1994). *Truth and Method*. Translated from German by J. Weinsheimer and D. G. Marshall. New York: Continuum.

Gao, Bingzhong. (2004). Zhishifenzi, minjian, yu yige simiao bowuguan de dansheng [Intellectuals, Local Society, the Birth of a Temple Museum]. *Mianjian Wenhua Forum*, 2004(3), 13–18.

Gao, Bingzhong. (2007). Zuowei feiwuzhi wenhuayichan yanjiu keti de minjian xinyang [Folk Beliefs as a Research Subject of Intangible Cultural Heritage]. *Jiangxi Social Sciences*, 2007(3), 146–154.

Gong, Shijian, Min Fang, and Rong Chang. (2015). Xuanyuan long yu gu, baidai jingxing tang. *People's Daily*, April 6 [online]. http://paper.people.com.cn/

rmrbhwb/html/2015-04/06/content_1550710.htm [accessed February 25, 2025] (in Chinese).

Guo, Yingjie. (2004). *Cultural Nationalism in Contemporary China: The Search for National Identity under Reform*. Abingdon: Routledge.

Handler, Richard. (1988). *Nationalism and the Politics of Culture in Quebec*. Madison: University of Wisconsin Press.

Handler, Richard. (2011). The "Ritualisation of Ritual" in the Construction of Heritage. In Christian Brosius and Karin M. Polit, eds., *Ritual, Heritage and Identity: The Politics of Culture and Performance in a Globalised World*. Abingdon: Routledge, pp. 39–54.

He, Nu. (2021). Zhai Taoshi Yizhizhong Xuzhao Yaoshun. Wenhua Zhongguo. *Guangmin News*, August 28 [online]. Available at: https://m.thepaper.cn/newsDetail_forward_14291021 [accessed 4 July 2024] (in Chinese).

He, Yingjie. (2023). Guimao nian lingbao huangdi zhudingyuan baizu dadian longzhong juban. *People's Daily Online*, April 22 [online]. Available at: https://mp.pdnews.cn/Pc/ArtInfoApi/article?id=35236908 [accessed April 7, 2024] (in Chinese).

Herzfeld, Michael. (1991). *A Place in History: Social and Monumental Time in a Cretan Town*. Princeton, NJ: Princeton University Press.

Herzfeld, Michael. (1997). *Portrait of a Greek Imagination: An Ethnographic Biography of Andreas Nenedakis*. Chicago, IL: Chicago University Press.

Herzfeld, Michael. (2004). *The Body Impolitic: Artisans and Artifice in the Global Hierarchy of Value*. Chicago, IL: University of Chicago Press.

Hobsbawm, Eric, and Terence Ranger, eds. (1983). *The Invention of Tradition*. Cambridge: Cambridge University Press.

Hu, Yicheng. (2017). Archaeological Presumption About the Upper and Lower Time Limits of the Yellow Emperor Period. Paper presented at the Annual Meeting of the Society of Shaanxi Xuanyuan Huangdi Seminar, Shaanxi (in Chinese).

Huang, Jin-Xing. (2015). The Symbolic Expansion of the Meaning and Function of the Rites of Confucian Temples in Imperial China. *Bulletin of the Institute of History and Philology Academia Sinica*, 86(3), 471–511 (in Chinese).

Jiang, Tao. (2023). Xing zou he nan ·Du dong zhong guo Tan mi ling bao huang di zhu ding yuan. *Henan Provincial Administration of Cultural Heritage*, January 11 [online]. Available at: https://wwj.henan.gov.cn/2023/01-11/2671236.html [accessed April 7, 2024] (in Chinese).

Jinba, Tenzin. (2013). *In the Land of the Eastern Queendom: The Politics of Gender and Ethnicity on the Sino-Tibetan Border*. Seattle: University of Washington Press.

Jing, Jun. (1996). T*he Temple of Memories: History, Power, and Morality in a Chinese Village*. Stanford, CA: Stanford University Press.

Johnson, Ian. (2017). *The Souls of China: The Return of Religion after Mao*. New York: Pantheon Books.

Koselleck, Reinhart. (1985). *Futures Past: On the Semantics of Historical Time*. Translated from German by Keith Tribe. Cambridge, MA: MIT Press.

Ku, Ming-chun. (2018). ICH-ization of Popular Religions and the Politics of Recognition in China. In Natsuko Akagawa and Laurajane Smith, eds., *Safeguarding Intangible Heritage: Practices and Politics*. Abingdon: Routledge, pp. 187–199.

Law of the People's Republic of China on Intangible Cultural Heritage. (2011). Beijing: Standing Committee of the National People's Congress.

Levenson, Joseph R. (1967). The Province, the Nation, and the World: The Problem of Chinese Identity. In Rhoads Murphey and Mary C. Wright, eds., *Approaches to Modern Chinese History*. Berkeley: University of California Press, pp. 268–288.

Li, Xinwei. (2010). Lingbao xipo yizhi de faxian yu sikao. *Chinese Social Sciences Today* (Beijing), February 2, 14.

Li, Xueqin. (2008). Gushi, kaoguxue yu yanhuang erdi. *New Legalist*, February 12 [online]. Available at: www.xinfajia.net/4162.html [accessed August 16, 2024] (in Chinese).

Liao, Yifang. (2016). On the Grounds and Implications of the Worship of Past Emperors in Medieval China. *Bulletin of the Institute of History and Philology, Academia Sinica*, 87(3), 507–568.

Lin, Chen-Yi. (2024). Haixia liangan gongji xuanyuan huangdi dadian Zhejiang jinyun juhang. *Udn.com*, April 16 [online]. Available at: https://udn.com/news/story/7332/7881120 [accessed April 7, 2024] (in Chinese).

Lin, Mei-Rong. (1988). From Religious Sphere to Belief Sphere: The Regional Composition and Development of Taiwanese Civil Society. In Yen Hsien Chang, ed., *China Maritime Development History Studies*, 3 vols. Taipei: Institute of the Three Principles of the People, Academia Sinica, pp. 95–125 (in Chinese).

Liu, Haifa. (2006). Huguang shanse shengxihu—xinmi huangdi gong. *Xinmi Municipal People's Government*, June 19 [online]. Available at: www.xinmi.gov.cn/zxdt/1356861.jhtml [accessed April 7, 2024] (in Chinese).

Liu, Li. (1999). Who Were the Ancestors? The Origins of Chinese Ancestral Cult and Racial Myths. *Antiquity*, 73(281), 602–613.

Liu, Long-Hsin. (2019). *Production and Dissemination of Knowledge: The Transformation of Modern Chinese Historiography*. Taipei: San Min Book Co. (in Chinese).

Madsen, Richard. (2014). From Socialist Ideology to Cultural Heritage: The Changing Basis of Legitimacy in the People's Republic of China. *Anthropology and Medicine*, 21(1), 58–70.

McNeal, Robin. (2012). Constructing Myth in Modern China. *Journal of Asian Studies*, 71(3), 679–704.

Lowenthal, David. (2018). *The Heritage Crusade and the Spoils of History.* Cambridge: Cambridge University Press.

McNeal, Robin. (2015). Moral Transformation and Local Identity: Reviving the Culture of Shun at Temples and Monuments across China. *Modern China*, 41(4), 436–464.

McNeal, Robin. (2021). Myth, Prayer, and Social Integration in Popular Chinese Religion: The Lingqiu Temple in Zhangzi County, Shanxi, and the Cult of the Daughter of Yandi. In Miao Zhe and Guolong Lai, eds., *Occult Arts, Art History and Cultural Exchange in Early China: Festschrift for Li Ling on the Occasion of His 70th Birthday.* Hangzhou: Zhejiang University Press.

Mon, Xi-An and Le-Wen Wang. (2004). Overseas Chinese and All Chinese Are Worshipping the Ancestor Yellow Emperor on the Tomb Sweeping Day: Worshipping Common Ancestor of China and Consolidating National Identity. *People's Daily*, March 24.

Oakes, Tim, and Donald S. Sutton. (2010). Introduction. In Tim Oakes and Donald S. Sutton, eds., *Faiths on Display: Religion, Tourism, and the Chinese State.* Lanham, MD: Rowman and Littlefield, pp. 1–25.

Olick, Jeffrey. (2007). *The Politics of Regret: On Collective Memory and Historical Responsibility.* New York: Routledge.

Sahlins, M. (1999). Two or Three Things That I Know About Culture. *Journal of the Royal Anthropological Institute*, 5(3), 399–421.

Sangren, P. Steven. (2000). *Chinese Sociologics: An Anthropological Account of the Role of Alienation in Social Reproduction.* London School of Economics Monographs on Social Anthropology No. 72. London: Athlone Press.

Sangren, P. Steven. (2017). *Filial Obsessions: Chinese Patriliny and Its Discontents.* Cham: Palgrave Macmillan.

Shen, Song-Qiao. (1997). The Myth of Huang-ti (the Yellow Emperor) and the Construction of Chinese Nationhood in Late Qing. *Taiwan: A Radical Quarterly in Social Studies*, 28, 1–77 (in Chinese).

Shen, Weilong. (2017). Huangdi Wenhua Xunzong: Yangguanzhai Shimao faxian de jishi. *Sohu News*, November 12 [online]. Available at: www.sohu .com/a/205643978_428863 [accessed April 7, 2024] (in Chinese).

Sima, Qian. (1996). *Record of the Grand Historian: Han Dynasty II*. Translated and edited by Burton Watson. New York: Columbia University Press.

Siu, Helen F. (1990). Recycling Tradition: Culture, History, and Political Economy in the Chrysanthemum Festivals of South China. *Comparative Studies in Society and History*, 32(4), 765–794.

State Council of the People's Republic of China. (2005a). *Notice of the State Council on Strengthening Cultural Heritage Protection*. Beijing: State Council of the People's Republic of China. Available at: https://zwgk.mct .gov.cn/zfxxgkml/zcfg/gfxwj/202012/t20201204_906080.html [accessed February 12, 2025] (in Chinese).

State Council of the People's Republic of China. (2005b). *Opinions of the State Council General Office on Strengthening the Protection of China's Intangible Cultural Heritage*. Beijing: State Council of the People's Republic of China. Available at: www.gov.cn/zwgk/2005-08/15/content_21681.htm [accessed February 12, 2025] (in Chinese).

Stewart, Charles. (2016). Historicity and Anthropology. *Annual Review of Anthropology*, 45(1), 79–94.

Su, Bingqi, and Weizhang Yin. (1981). Questions Relating to the Distribution and Development of Regional Culture in Archaeology. *Wenwu*, 5, 10–17 (in Chinese).

Sun, Longji. (2000). Late Qing Nationalism and the Invention of the Cult of the Yellow Emperor. *Historical Research*, 2000(3), 68–79 (in Chinese).

Thompson, Thomas L. (2014). *Biblical Narrative and Palestine's History: Changing Perspectives 2*. New York: Routledge.

Trigger, Bruce G. (1995). Romanticism, Nationalism, and Archaeology. In Philip L. Kohl and Clare Fawcett, eds., *Nationalism, Politics, and the Practice of Archaeology*. Cambridge: Cambridge University Press, pp. 263–279.

Von Falkenhausen, Lothar. (1993). On the Historiographical Orientation of Chinese Archaeology. *Antiquity*, 67(257), 839–849.

Von Falkenhausen, Lothar. (1995). The Regionalist Paradigm in Chinese Archaeology. In Philip L. Kohl and Clare P. Fawcett, eds., *Nationalism, Politics, and the Practice of Archaeology*. Cambridge: Cambridge University Press, pp. 198–217.

Wagner, Rudolf G. (2019). The Global Context of a Modern Chinese Quandary. *Monumenta Serica*, 67(2), 441–504.

Walsh, Kevin. (1992). *The Representation of the Past: Museums and Heritage in the Post-Modern World*. Abingdon: Routledge.

Wang, Ming-ke. (2002). The Ancient Foundations of Modern Nation-Building in China: The Case of the Offering of Yan and Yellow Emperors. *Bulletin of IHP [Institute of History and Philology]*, 73(3), 583–624 (in Chinese).

Wang, Shu-Li. (2016). Civilization and the Transformation of Xiaotun Village at China's Yinxu Archaeological Site. In Christoph Brumann and David Berliner, eds., *World Heritage on the Ground: Ethnographic Perspectives*. New York: Berghahn Books, pp. 171–192.

Wang, Shu-Li. (2021). Who Owns the Culture of the Yellow Emperor? In Shu-Li Wang, Michael Rowlands, and Yujie Zhu, eds., *Heritage and Religion in East Asia*. Abingdon: Routledge, pp. 32–52.

Wang, Shu-Li, and Michael Rowlands. (2017). Making and Unmaking Heritage Values in China. In Haidy Geismar and Jane Anderson, eds., *The Routledge Companion to Cultural Property*. New York: Routledge, pp. 258–274.

Wang, Syu-Ruei. (2006). The Huangdi Worship: Official Huangdi Worship and Folk Huangdi Worship. Master's thesis, Minzu University of China.

Wang, Yun. (2021). Zhongguo dalu zhongjia zhongguohua xinyang xianzhuang yu chongtu. *Jiaoliu Magazine, Straits Exchange Foundation*, June, 177 [online]. Available at: www.sef.org.tw/article-1-129-12915 [accessed April 7, 2024] (in Chinese).

Watson, James L. (1985). Standardizing the Gods: The Promotion of T'ien Hou (Empress of Heaven) along the South China Coast 960–1960. In David Johnson, Andrew Nathan, and Evelyn Rawski, eds., *Popular Culture in Late Imperial China*. Berkeley: University of California Press, pp. 292–324.

Wu, Zhen. (2009). Cong fengjian mixin dao feiwuzhi wenhua yichan: minjian Xinyang de hefaxing licheng [From Feudal Superstition to Intangible Cultural Heritage: The Legitimization of Folk Beliefs]. In Ze Jin and Yonghui Qiu, eds., *Zongjiao lanpishu: Zhongguo Zongjiao Baogao*. Beijing: Shehui kexue wenxian chubanshe, pp. 161–180.

Xiao, yu, Shen Bin, and Liu Xiao-Ling. (2022). Lishui Jinyun Huangdi wenhua fengfu Zhejiang wenhua biaoshi xinneihan. *People's Daily Online*, June 27 [online]. Available at: http://zj.people.com.cn/BIG5/n2/2022/0627/c186327-40013189.html [accessed April 7, 2024] (in Chinese).

Xie, Jiajun, and Fengli Wang. (2023). Lishui chutu guojia erji zhengui wenwu beisong jinlong Jinyi bushi zheng "xian dou dong tian" diwei he huangdi jisi lishi. *People's Daily Online*, January 28 [online]. Available at: http://zj.people.com.cn/BIG5/n2/2023/0128/c186327-40279500.html [accessed April 7, 2024] (in Chinese).

Xinhua News Agency. (2021). Xi Jingping zai guanguo zhongjia gongzuohuiyi shang qiangdiao jianchi woguo zhongjia zhongguohua fangxiang. *Xinhua Net*, December 4 [online]. Available at: www.news.cn/2021-12/04/c_1128131454.htm [accessed December 1, 2024] (in Chinese).

Xu, Chialu. (2015). Promoting the Huangdi Ceremony to a National Ceremony. *GuangMing Daily*, September 7 [online]. Available at: http://epaper.gmw.cn/gmrb/html/2015-09/07/nw.D110000g-mrb_20150907_1-16.htm [accessed January 1, 2019] (in Chinese).

Yan, Haiming. (2018). *World Heritage Craze in China: Universal Discourse, National Culture and Local Memory*. New York: Berghahn Books.

Yang, Dayong, and Li Kan. (2024). Henansheng zhengxie weiyuan jianyi: zai lingbao Huangdi zhudingyuan she baizu fenhuichang. *China News Service*, January 29 [online]. Available at: https://m.chinanews.com/wap/detail/cht/zw/ft10154777.shtml [accessed April 7, 2024] (in Chinese).

Yang, Jui-Sung. (2010). *Sick Man, Yellow Peril and Sleeping Lion: Chinese Images from "Western" Perspective and the Discourses of Modern Chinese National Identity*. Taipei: Chengchi University Press (in Chinese).

Zhu, Yujie. (2018). *Heritage and Romantic Consumption in China*. Amsterdam: Amsterdam University Press.

Zhu, Yujie, and Christina Maags. (2020). *Heritage Politics in China: The Power of the Past*. Abingdon: Routledge.

# Acknowledgment

I extend my gratitude to the series editor and the two reviewers for their valuable comments. I am also deeply thankful to the friends who facilitated my fieldwork in Henan, Shaanxi, and Zhejiang, as well as to my dedicated research assistants, MA Chen-han, CHENG Yu-chun, CHU Fang-I, and WANG An-yan. This research was funded by the National Science Council in Taiwan (MOST109-2410-H001-011-MY3).

# Cambridge Elements

## Critical Heritage Studies

Kristian Kristiansen
*University of Gothenburg*

Michael Rowlands
*UCL*

### About the Series

This series focuses on the recently established field of Critical Heritage Studies. Interdisciplinary in character, it brings together contributions from experts working in a range of fields, including cultural management, anthropology, archaeology, politics, and law. The series will include volumes that demonstrate the impact of contemporary theoretical discourses on heritage found throughout the world, raising awareness of the acute relevance of critically analysing and understanding the way heritage is used today to form new futures.

www.ingramcontent.com/pod-product-compliance
Ingram Content Group UK Ltd.
Pitfield, Milton Keynes, MK11 3LW, UK
UKHW021825260525
458789UK00012B/110